HEY KID!

HEY KID!

A Tiger Batboy Remembers

DANNY DILLMAN

iUniverse, Inc.
New York Lincoln Shanghai

Hey Kid!
A Tiger Batboy Remembers

iUniverse books may be ordered through booksellers or by contacting:

iUniverse
2021 Pine Lake Road, Suite 100
Lincoln, NE 68512
www.iuniverse.com
1-800-Authors (1-800-288-4677)

ISBN-13: 978-0-595-41849-7 (pbk)
ISBN-13: 978-0-595-86194-1 (ebk)
ISBN-10: 0-595-41849-X (pbk)
ISBN-10: 0-595-86194-6 (ebk)

Printed in the United States of America

List of Illustrations

Eddie Waitkus

Ted Williams

The above photographs were obtained with the kind permission of the National Baseball Hall of Fame Library photo department, Cooperstown, New York.

Floor plan of the visitor's clubhouse, Briggs Stadium, 1948 to 1950 (created from personal notes).

The place was Detroit, Michigan. The site was Briggs Stadium, the home of the Detroit Tigers. The moment was every series. There was Danny Dillman, the batboy in the visitor's dugout. Everybody in our school wanted his job (other schools also)—"the dream job."

I have known Danny Dillman for 50 plus years. Both as a teammate and a personal friend at Northwestern High School in Detroit, Michigan, and later at Northern Illinois University in DeKalb, Illinois.

We started as teammates at Northwestern High School in Detroit, Michigan. We were West Side Champions and City Runners Up. Fifty years later we are able to look at the inside of the game—in the clubhouse and in the dugout. His book explains the inner working parts of baseball life, before the game, during the game, after the game, and as he witnessed the beginning of integration.

I played for Northwestern High School and coach Sam Bishop; Detroit Stars in the Negro League (Detroit Stars), Ted Rasberry, Detroit Pepsi Cola National Champs and later returned to coach at Northwestern High School (where Willie Horton and Alex Johnson, American League batting champion were just two of the fine players).

Danny, Distinguished Teaching Professor Emeritus, coached in the Little League program in DeKalb, Illinois, using knowledge from Sam Bishop, the legendary coach from Detroit, and all the American League teams and coaches of the era—1948-49-50.

I urged Dan to write this book—as did many others.

Danny met the icons of baseball—Joe DiMaggio, Ted Williams, Bob Feller and Larry Doby, Dominic DiMaggio, Luke Easter—wow—Danny, tell us more.

Friend, teammate, and colleague,

Walter Owens
Assistant Professor
Kinesiology and Physical Education
Former Assistant Basketball Coach
Former Head Baseball Coach
Northern Illinois University

Contents

Preface

"Old batboys never die, they just forget
where the bat rack is."—Anonymous

I began to write this book three years ago when the Detroit Tigers again were mired in last place in the American League's Central Division. Their ineptitude on the playing field forced me to recall happier days when the Bengals were competitive with the Red Sox, Yankees, and Indians. I was surprised how easily images and events from the past returned to cheer me decades later. Other books recounting experiences similar to mine at Briggs (Tiger) Stadium failed to provide satisfactory models for what I wanted to share with readers. I chose instead to use an episodic format to describe a series of circumstances in my three years as batboy for visiting teams in the late forties and early fifties—1948 to 1950. The book is not so much about my day-to-day life as batboy as it is about what I witnessed and what I learned about baseball on the field and in the clubhouse at the corner of Michigan and Trumbull Avenues. For three years I had the greatest job a kid could have as I discovered the complexities of an apparently simple game.

Major league baseball passed through important changes after World War II, and I was there unobtrusively to make note for later recall. The color line was broken, new batting styles became popular, and ballparks altered their appearances. As batboy I was present for the first of these changes, and I closely watched the others as a fan in the grandstand. As years passed continued study of the game led to better understanding of the players who had used the visitor's clubhouse in Detroit when I was a teenager. Baseball fans will find fresh viewpoints of an earlier time that is less familiar to people who follow the game today. If you recognize any anecdotes, remember, I heard them first. Some conversations among players represent a summary of interactions among them during a three year period. If some readers flinch at the lack of political correctness with respect to ethnic and racial references, they should permit me to reproduce language as often spoken in the clubhouse and on the field. The ballpark was not a polite gentlemen's club. I discovered that my heroes were not as heroic as I had imagined. They had failings like everyone else. This revelation failed to erase my affection for the game; it created a more mature perspective . Enjoy.

Acknowledgements

Authors don't write books alone. Many people assist in different ways. Some offer encouragement and a willingness to read and to criticize preliminary drafts. Others help by supplying photographs and compiling statistics. Still others educate writers in the mysteries of the computer and even set aside valuable time to type manuscript copy. Each of these individuals not only make a book possible but make it better than it would have been without their involvement. For this book it is necessary to identify especially the following people who shared my enthusiasm for *Hey Kid!*:

Joanne, my wife, for her patient and diligent preparation of the manuscript;

Richard Quinney, my dear friend, for early and unwavering support;

Amy Polzin for an outstanding job in preparing a huge body of player stats;

Christina Gilleran, former student, for critically reading the manuscript while she wrote a memoir of her own;

The very helpful people in the photo and media sales department at the Hall of Fame in Cooperstown, New York, particularly John Horn in photo sales;

Len Walther, NIU Geography Department, for creating the floor plan of the Visitor's Clubhouse at Briggs Stadium from my drawings;

Mark Howland, NIU Geology Department, for helping to create the cover design and for taking my picture for the back cover.

Thanks to all.

Daniel Dillman
Fall, 2006

Chapter 1

Horse Droppings in the Alley

"Baseball is a ballet without music. Drama without words.
A carnival without kewpie dolls"—Ernie Harwell's 1955
Opening Day essay in the *Sporting News*, entitled "The Game
For all America."

In September 1999 the Detroit Tigers played their final games in Tiger Stadium (Briggs Stadium, Navin Field, Bennett Field). Co-America Park would be their new home downtown about a mile away from the site where major league baseball had been played longer than at any other. My sons, Christien and Evan, wanted to share with me one last experience at the old ball yard at Michigan and Trumbull Avenues, so they had called the Tiger community relations office and asked if anything special could be arranged for an old batboy attending his last game "on the corner."

I was thrilled by the possibility of once more seeing the place where my life changed so dramatically when I was a teenager. The opportunity to bond with my sons in this way was not to be missed, because they each had growing families and seldom had time for such an adventure. During the 1940s and 1950s, Tiger Stadium was called Briggs Stadium after the team's owner, Walter O. Briggs. The ball yard at the corner of Michigan and Trumbull Avenues previously had been named after an earlier owner, Frank Navin, and before that a 19th century catcher, Charlie Bennett. Names changed, but the location of the playing field remained the same. The Tigers became identified with one corner of the intersection of Michigan and Trumbull Avenues, which carried important street car lines until after mid-20th century. The phrase—baseball at the corner—eventually became synonymous with Tiger baseball in Detroit. T-shirts carried the phrase with a likeness of the stadium as a popular logo. 'Save the stadium' groups even used it as a part of their message to preserve the venerable structure in the 1990s.

Little did I realize then, that a visit to the corner of Michigan and Trumbull Avenues would revive so many pleasant memories. The three years from 1948-1950 became instantly real again when the old ballpark stood before us clothed in bright white paint with the old English D Tiger logo on the walls. We went through the tour group entrance on Michigan Ave., and I immediately began to describe for the boys what we would see inside. I paid little attention to the tour guide, as my excitement increased with each step. I had my own story to tell. Christien and Evan were surprised that I remembered so much detail about my former work place after 49 years. We never again would experience the sounds and smells of this classic old ballpark getting ready for a day's game. But if I had been sightless, I could have told the boys our exact position. The only new smell came from the concession stands preparing slabs of pizza, America's staff of life.

We eventually were separated from the main body of the tour group for our "special" experience. We paused in the upper deck grandstand in right field and in left field, before going down to the bullpens in deep center field. The boys stared in disbelief at the tall iconic flagpole near the home bullpen gate over 400 feet from home plate. What happened if a batted ball hit the pole, they asked? I explained that the ball was in play, and I twice had seen a ball carom off the pole. By now they were converted to preservation of Tiger Stadium. Our last stop on the memorable tour was the visiting team's dugout. So many happy memories flooded back as I looked into the dugout, where my former perch on the steps near the drinking fountain and the bat rack greeted me as though I had never left. We all agreed the trip had been worth every penny.

Several hours later, we were in good seats behind the Minnesota Twins bullpen in right field. The Tigers rose to the occasion by playing well and edged the Twins 2-0. Before the seventh inning stretch, a group of half a dozen young people from public relations arrived at our seats to serenade me with "For He's a Jolly Good Fellow" and to present me with a sack full of mementos, much to the surprise of everyone around us. A drunken young woman seated nearby loudly exclaimed to her equally trashed friends—in slurred speech, "Who the hell is he? Why's he getting all that shit?" The nostalgia of the moment ended abruptly with that sincere expression of envy, yet I couldn't forget that over fifty years ago I had realized every boy's dream—to be a batboy for his heroes. As we returned to Detroit Metropolitan Airport after the game for the flight home, I relived those early games in the alleys of the inner city when I hoped to some day play for the Tigers.

Inner city kids lacking playgrounds in Detroit often were forced to find recreational space in the alleys. Many people staying in the Astor Court Apartments on West Grand Boulevard (across from Henry Ford Hospital), where my family spent ten years, were transients with few or no kids to play ball. There were only four of us, two boys and two girls, who were the perennials for touch football, but mostly for baseball. Rawboned, scholarly George was several years ahead of me in school and never without a plastic pocket container for his pens and pencils. In college his best friend would be his slide rule when he studied engineering at Michigan Technological University. Tall, slim and willowy, Barbara had long brown hair and also was older and wiser about the ways of the world. No doubt she became a stunningly attractive mature woman. And finally, there was sweet Sally, who was younger, more compact and shapely than Barbara and had short wavy blond hair. George and I were very fortunate to have had such pretty companions who liked to play baseball—with boys. They threw and hit as well as any boys their age. No allowance was made for gender difference. In fact sometimes Barb and Sally kicked our butts good and gleefully taunted us for the rest of the week. Oddly, I can't remember one time when any of the four fathers appeared in the alley to mentor their kids on the finer points of the game. George and Barbara's dads were completely uninterested. Sally's father got his exercise by walking the family Dalmatian. My dad was a traveling salesman and away for long periods of time and lacked athletic ability.

Our games were interrupted only by homework, Sundays, and occasional family trips and vacations. But the most abrupt disruption occurred when my passion for baseball got the better of good judgment in answering calls of nature. If we took a break, George went to the seventh floor, Barb and I went to the fifth floor, and Sally returned to the fourth floor. A quick trip to the fifth floor meant waiting for the elevator, then running down a short hallway, then a long one, the length of the building. One day when I was wearing my replica of a Tiger uniform, I was forced to leave the "playing field" quickly. A leap upward to snag a ball hit over my head resulted in loss of control over my bowels. Suddenly, the crotch of my beloved uniform pants were filled with poop. The elevator ride to the fifth floor was even more embarrassing because people kept getting on at each floor! My stressful condition was obvious to each new arrival in the elevator, yet no one offered a sympathetic word! Maybe the worst part of this trip to my apartment was the long hallway route. Running was impossible because much of what had been in the crotch of the uniform succumbed to gravity and fell down each leg coming to rest at the bottom of the pants tucked into uniform socks!! The afternoon ended as my mother, aghast at my appearance and my odor, insisted on hosing me down in the bathtub. All future sessions of ball playing were coordinated more carefully with physical needs, once my uniform was ready again for competition.

I was convinced, however, that my efforts to become a professional baseball player had suffered a huge setback. Major league players certainly didn't shit their pants! Actually, several years later, an outfielder for the Washington Senators would call time during a game, then run full throttle to the dugout, bound down the dugout steps, speed through the tunnel heading for the clubhouse toilet, and frantically drop his uniform pants, just as he arrived not a second too soon. Teammates were convulsed with laughter and offered no sympathy for his discomfort. I had thought only dumb kids filled their pants while playing. I was almost right.

Playing ball with two pretty teenage girls had both advantages and disadvantages. Their skill level was competitive with boys their age but the girls advancing physical maturity could be distracting, especially for teenage boys with raging hormones. The girls were not reluctant to tease and to raise expectations of what might be possible—but always at the wrong time. A trip down in the elevator with arms made immovable by bats, balls, and gloves suddenly became a darkened journey when the overhead light went off and soft lips touched lightly in the darkness. Was it Barb or Sally? Identities could be traced to the smell of bath soap or light perfume. Crowded elevators conveniently forced the girls against the boys, an opportunity for the girls to move seductively and cause uncontrollable physical responses by male bodies. I needed help to carry our equipment out of the elevator because I had to hold my glove in front of me to hide obvious signs of my excitement. The girls giggled at the visible results of their teasing. They usually had little difficulty in scoring the most runs after such an episode quickly weakened my attempt to seriously concentrate on a game of alley baseball.

Baseball always was my favorite sport, either as a participant, or vicariously, when I created my own fantasy league and calculated batting averages, earned run averages and traded players from team to team. Playing baseball in paved alleys of inner city Detroit during the mid- and late 1940s was, to say the least, an exciting challenge. Unable to mark off a real diamond with three bases, the hardy band of mixed gender kids in my apartment building instead, without knowing it, reinvented the one ol' cat version of baseball. In other words, we had home plate and a convenient telephone pole serving as first base. The batter hit the pitched ball down the slot of the narrow alley, then ran back and forth between the telephone pole and home plate until the ball, if not caught on the fly, arrived back to the pitcher. One round trip, pole to plate, put a runner on second base, two round trips meant a homerun.

Balls deteriorated rapidly, however, as the concrete surface took its toll. Soon, almost any of us were able to hit the loosened cover off the ball. Enter friction tape as an emergency and cheaper substitute for horsehide. The unforgiving hard alley surface altered the tools of the game in other ways, namely, choosing sides. Swinging a bat and dropping it before scampering for the telephone pole quickly broke off the knob of the bat handle. It was impossible to claim "eagle claws" around the knob, when hand after hand was placed upward around the handle of the bat that had been tossed from one person to another in preparation for forming teams. Still other obstacles hindered our play; jagged nails jutting out from garage doors, uneven sewer drain openings in the alley floor, apartment house windows inviting wickedly powerful line drives, high-tension wires between utility poles, parked cars eagerly awaiting the daily collection of dents, and most challenging of all—horse droppings.

Remember that in the 1940s milk deliveries to houses and apartment buildings were made by horse-drawn wagons. The milkman supplied a range of dairy products and block ice for iceboxes. At each apartment house stop along the way, horses were left to stand in the alley with oat bags attached to their muzzles while the milkman went from floor to floor—as many as eight floors in my building with sixteen apartments per floor. While the milkman labored, his horse defecated in copious amounts and formed dung piles of, at times, grand dimensions. The players in a game of one ol' cat were forced to make instantaneous decisions when playing on such a surface dotted with mounds of sweet-smelling horseshit. Was catching and throwing the ball back to the pitcher really important when the ball was smeared with dung? You never used your glove after the milkman's visit. It was far better to have feces on your hands than on your glove. Batters also faced a moment of truth when they stepped to the plate following milk deliveries. Swing or not to swing? It always was high comedy (at least for the pitcher) to switch balls before delivering the pitch and to serve up a dung ball over the heart of the plate that was too inviting for the batter to pass up. Splitter, splatter and raucous laughter. Usually the two guys pulled this stunt on each other and the two girls likewise. We all saw the choice of gender target as an expression of politeness. But, perhaps, even more as a means to keep our small group together. No doubt the four mothers often starred in disbelief when their children returned from the playing field in need of a thorough hosing down. Perhaps I had more to lose eventually on each game day than my three dear friends. I insisted on wearing my Tiger uniform and instantly became the object of taunting and derision. Even the two girls now anxiously awaited their turn to pitch, hoping that the Old English "D" on the uniform might somehow become emblazoned with an equine glob. For the most part, my charm prevailed, and I only got splattered twice.

But these carefree days with my apartment house friends George, Barbara, and Sally were destined to end. The girls moved away and my parents relocated in the neighborhood to a duplex inconveniently located away from the alley playing field. In another sense, the four of us had outgrown our recreational space. We were all in high school with new interests and priorities—except for me.

Baseball became a part of me, as with many people my age, by way of radio broadcasts during the WWII years. President Franklin Roosevelt used major league baseball as a means to boost morale from 1942-1945. First in Detroit, I listened to Ty Tyson, whose effective use of silence and pause in his delivery set him apart from others describing the game. When my family returned to southern Illinois for summer vacations, I picked up the night broadcasts of the St. Louis Cardinals and the St. Louis Browns. Night baseball was a necessity then and still is in the suffocating heat of St. Louis. In addition to following the Tigers, the two teams from Missouri commanded the attention of a young boy. No one in Detroit understood my affection for the lovable losers in brown uniforms and caps, who even managed to reach the World Series in 1944. The St .Louis Browns won their only pennant that year but lost to the Cardinals in the World Series. But in the days of an eight-team American League, every team had a few good players, the Browns included. In later years, I treasured the autographs of Walt Judnich, Jeff Heath, and Chet Laabs, who were hard-hitting outfielders for the often woeful Brownies.

After the Tigers victory in the 1945 World Series, baseball fever swept over Detroit. Everyone followed the fortunes of the snarling Bengals. Meanwhile, skinny, sickly Danny Dillman began to lift weights, drink a quart of milk daily, eat plenty of Wheaties and a pound of bacon for breakfast, when possible. I went to Palmer Park, about three miles away near Woodward Avenue, on weekends with my dad. He hit grounders and fly balls to me until he tired long before I was ready to quit. I knew that I also needed a strong throwing arm in order to make it to the big leagues.

I practiced long throws in the alley next to Astor Court Apartments to strengthen my arm, and I tried to pitch to my friend George wherever we found open space—even along the sidewalk in front of the Presbyterian Church, which proved to be a poor choice of location for a bullpen. One day I expertly destroyed the plate glass in the church's sign with a curve ball that didn't. The sign advised the neighborhood about the importance of telling the truth. I had no choice but to fess up and offer to help with sweeping and other cleaning jobs for Sundays. As it turned out pushing a holy broom was good training for the visitor's clubhouse at Briggs Stadium.

A summer day's journey to Briggs Stadium by streetcar or bus passed through corridors filled with the voice of Harry Heilmann, the Tigers popular broadcaster. He was said by many to have been one of the two greatest right-handed hitters in history. Before air conditioning and television, you could follow the progress of the day's game with Harry from one neighborhood to another, from shop to shop, and house to house, as open windows and doors poured the sound of baseball into the streets. Heilmann's calling of the game was more a sequence of anecdotes than a faithful description of events. Yet for a few years, he was as beloved to Detroit fans as Harry Caray would be in St. Louis and in Chicago. His premature departure from the broadcast booth due to illness changed forever the summer day personality of the best baseball town in America as society, and the game entered a new phase in the Motor City.

In the winter of 1948 the Detroit Tigers used an essay contest to select teenage boys to work in the visitor's clubhouse as batboys and clubhouse boys. At that time, the American League had the following seven teams in addition to the Tigers: New York Yankees; Boston Red Sox (known as the Dead Sox when their bats fell silent on long road trips); Cleveland Indians; Philadelphia Athletics; Chicago White Sox; St. Louis Browns; and Washington Senators (first in war, first in peace, and last in the American League). This was the opportunity of a lifetime. Imagine being with my heroes for 77 home games!!! I crafted the best essay I could and laced it with exaggerated comments about my ability to run fast, to throw far, and to accept any task willingly. Passing days seemed to confirm that my entry must have been lousy, unacceptable, if not unread. I decided that something else was needed to focus attention on me and not the other equally eager boys. Immediately I set to work, drawing a likeness of former umpire and now general manager of the Tigers, Billy Evans. Might as well go to the top where decisions were made! When the telephone finally rang weeks later and the voice on the other end invited me to come to Briggs Stadium for an interview, I choked with excitement. The interview consisted of casual small-talk and several specific questions about the need to arrange with my high school principal to have all my classes completed by noon. Tiger home games, especially during the week, began at 3:00. And then, one final question, "If you can draw so well, (Billy Evans picture) why the hell would you want to work here for $3.00 a game?" My answer was a no-brainer. EVERYONE who applied for these jobs would have worked for nothing.

If the selection process was lengthy, the wait for opening day 1948 seemed endless. Yet it was much easier being patient when celebrity had been achieved. My classmates at Northwestern High School thought I was the luckiest kid on earth. Not only would I be mingling with the likes of Joe DiMaggio, Ted Williams, Hal Newhouser, and Larry Doby, but even better I would finish classes around 11:30 and leave for the ballpark. It was considered cool to be seen walking to class with me, and dates were much easier to get as a freshman. Even junior and senior girls knew Danny the Batboy. But newly found notoriety among my peers failed to give me complete confidence to go to the big leagues. On opening day 1948 my streetcar rattled along Trumbull Avenue through increasingly more modest neighborhoods. I wondered whether the other passengers on this chilly and cloudy day could see how nervous I was. My sandwich tasted like cardboard, and I could only manage to choke down a few bites of apple, because several bodily urges captured my thoughts. Either I would vomit the hastily eaten sandwich, or wet my pants, or both! How does a 14-year old boy control his emotions at a time like this? Within moments I would be inside a major league clubhouse.

Chapter 2

Jerry Coleman's Dirty Socks

"Winfield goes back to the wall. He hits his head on the
wall and it rolls off! It's rolling all the way back to
second base. This is a terrible thing for the Padres!"
Probably the most memorable Colemanism as broadcaster
for the San Diego Padres. See *"Legends of the Err Waves"*
By William Taaffe, *Sports Illustrated*, May 20, 1985.

The visitor's clubhouse was nestled in the bowels of Briggs Stadium conveniently across from a concession stand supplying ballpark franks and a variety of high carbohydrate treats. A sign prominently displayed next to the sliding door of the clubhouse aggressively communicated an example of irrefutable baseball logic— VISITOR'S CLUBHOUSE—NO VISITORS ALLOWED! With a total lack of confidence that I belonged there, I knocked softly, not wanting to intrude into the 'bigs', or the major leagues.

After several moments the door slid slowly open and Fat Frank covered the hole in the wall protected by the door. "Are you going to stand out there all day, or come in here and work?" was his friendly greeting to a teenaged boy so nervous he could barely speak. The clubhouse man was to be my boss, my mentor, and my critic for the next several years. The man's girth made rapid movement impossible and, as I often would observe, his consumption of candy bars and roast beef sandwiches eliminated any possibility of improved mobility. Once my all-consuming nervousness subsided, I began to realize that his daily movements away from his stool, which was located next to a cabinet filled with articles intended for sale to the ball players, might only be to defecate and to urinate.

Fat Frank was a man of few words and his first conversation with me, if one person speaking to another without reply can be called a conversation, began with: "O.K., here's the drill. You're probably scared shitless, but listen up and don't forget. This is the best visitor's clubhouse in the American League. All the players say so. That means you don't fuck up. Learn your responsibilities. Do without being told. If you don't pull your weight around here doing the work, I'll know, and your ass is gone! Understand?" A new phase of my life began at that moment, and I hadn't yet seen my heroes who would soon arrive. During my first year as batboy, I would anxiously await each team's first visit. I soon would see players whose stats I had been memorizing and whose exploits I had been hearing about on the radio.

The visitor's clubhouse at Briggs Stadium was an elongated, rectangular-shaped room. At the far end, toilets were in one corner, showers in the other, sinks were in between. Player's lockers were placed along the longest wall at the left. The trainer's room was adjacent to the showers and more lockers continued along the wall at the right, forming a U-shaped area across the front wall, broken only by the drying room, where wet wool flannel uniforms, socks and undergarments were hung after games. The middle of the clubhouse remained an open space for equipment trunks, which contained individual boxes with personal items for each player, plus bats, balls, "the tools of ignorance" (chest protectors, masks, and shin guards) for the catchers—everything the team would need on a short or lengthy road trip. Trunks arrived at the clubhouse in cartage vehicles after being picked up at the railway station. The late 1940s and early 1950s were years of rail, not air travel, by eight teams playing 77 road games and the same number of home games. Only the Yankees increasingly began to use travel by air in the years immediately following World War II.

Trunks were unpacked and player's personal boxes were put into their favorite lockers. This was not a random distribution. The best visitor's clubhouse in the American League made sure to put each player where he wanted to be and where he had been in previous visits, not next to someone with whom he was feuding, "Careful where you put the rookies, kid!" Fat Frank reminded me. "Some veterans won't sit near them. Remember DiMaggio and Williams are always toward the end on the left side, managers and coaches on the left side of the U-shaped locker area up front."

Unpacking trunks and hanging uniforms in the lockers were just two of the many clubhouse responsibilities for the batboys. If you wanted a job that required long hours doing laundry, folding towels, shining shoes, mopping floors, swabbing toilets, cleaning sinks and showers, handling sweaty uniforms, sanitary socks, jock straps and sweatshirts, running errands, carrying luggage and repacking equipment boxes, then you wanted to be a batboy. These were some of the mundane chores

Visitor's Clubhouse
Briggs Stadium

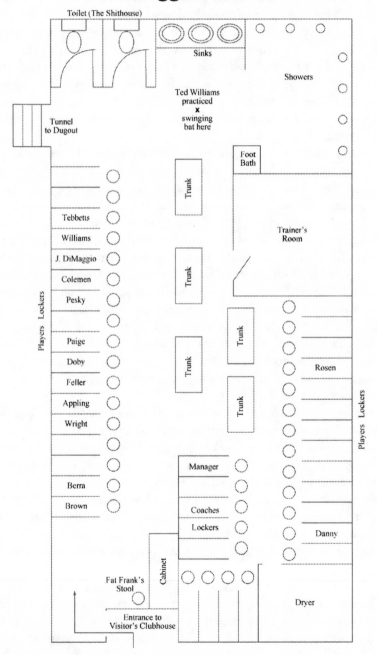

Toilet (The Shithouse)

Sinks

Showers

Ted Williams
practiced
x
swinging
bat here

Tunnel
to Dugout

Foot
Bath

Trunk

Trainer's
Room

Players Lockers

Tebbetts

Williams

J. DiMaggio

Colemen

Pesky

Paige

Doby

Feller

Appling

Wright

Berra

Brown

Trunk

Trunk

Trunk

Trunk

Trunk

Rosen

Players Lockers

Manager

Coaches

Lockers

Cabinet

Fat Frank's
Stool

Danny

Dryer

Entrance to
Visitor's Clubhouse

that needed to be done before batboys appeared in the dugout and on the playing field to carry bats and to chase foul balls. Here was the perfect low-paying entry-level position with no opportunity for advancement for young boys whose heroes were grown men playing a kid's game.

The clubhouse had glistening white and black tile walls with narrow pebble glass windows along the top of the wall, between the trainer's room and the clothes dryer. This was before the age of air conditioning and during the hottest, muggiest days of summer, comfort was provided partially by several floor fans. In July and August the fans only managed to circulate the hot moist air without much effective cooling. Although some players would shave and shower quickly after a game in order to escape the heat, others consumed enough beer (team rules permitting) to force at least another hour of free flowing perspiration, which did nothing to improve the foul smelling air in the room. Needless to say, the batboys didn't look forward to doing their chores in the dank atmosphere. We knew that the next morning the clubhouse air would smell like thirty stale armpits. All of the boys dreaded team departure in these conditions, after a night game or a double header. A huge amount of physical labor was required to load equipment and to stuff each player's personal items box with sweaty, dirty uniforms, sweatshirts, jockstraps, spikes (just knock the dirt off and jam them into the box), shaving kits and other items. Don't leave anything behind. Remember this is the best clubhouse in the American League!

Before the appearance of the boom box, major league clubhouses usually were quiet with only occasional laughter, and radios seldom provided entertainment except in the trainer's room—often used as a refuge from inquiring reporters. I easily could hear a player at the other end of the room call out, "Hey Kid," when I was needed for an errand or a quick clubhouse chore. There was surprisingly little interaction between managers and players. Coaches reviewed with starting pitchers and their catchers the preferred selection and sequence of pitches for Tiger hitters to be faced in the upcoming three or four-game series. Card playing before games was infrequent, most managers in the 1948-50 era seemed not to approve of the pastime, and the crowded clubhouse lacked adequate space for table and chairs. I remember being surprised that the noise level of the clubhouse was much lower than in my high school locker room.

In many clubhouses around the league the standard warning was clearly posted and understood by all. **"What you see here, what you hear here, what you say here, what you do here, let stay here, when you leave here."** The passage of more than 50 years, however, relaxes the intensity of these instructions. Many players are no longer with us, and baseball fans enjoy a glimpse into baseball's inner sanctum where they, themselves, would have loved to be. There probably has been little change in clubhouse conversation and humor over the years. Common elements were, and probably still are: sex, women, booze, sex, baseball and other sports gossip, who's slumping and who's streaking, sex, latest possessions acquired, when the new Cadillacs are scheduled to appear, the whereabouts of a good place to eat after the game, and sex. Deep thoughts were notable by their absence.

My mother frequently cautioned that if I wanted to grow up and join my heroes in the major leagues, I shouldn't smoke, drink, or carouse with women, but I should drink plenty of milk and eat my Wheaties. She was wrong on all counts. I soon discovered in the visitor's clubhouse that my heroes were not as heroic as I had imagined. They were pretty much like other people, except that in the late '40s and early '50s, ballplayers typically were from a rural southern background. Not only were polysyllable words infrequent, but, innovative uses of "fuck" were rampant, as the word easily became noun, verb, and adjective for many players to express themselves among their peers. The monotony of long road trips by rail (for example New York to St. Louis, Chicago, Cleveland, and Detroit) became obvious in the clubhouse where the range of activities was also limited. Some players always arrived early. Others spent as little time in the clubhouse as management allowed. Some would remove only their suit coat upon arrival and then quickly begin reading the newspaper before donning a uniform for batting practice. Keep in mind that this was a more formal public time in America. Most ball clubs required players to appear in public wearing suit and tie or jacket and tie. Many ball players wore hats (fedoras). This was the age of two-color wing-tipped shoes (black/white, brown/white) during the warmer months. Although even the finest tailoring failed to disguise bulky bodies, ball players resembled far more closely the successful businessman than today's proudly casual athletes, draped with gold chains.

Players typically would parade around the clubhouse in jockstraps, sweatshirts, and shower clogs as they went through their pre-game rituals. Some ball clubs allowed card games before games and beer afterward. The more conservative managers did not. Repetitive and dull hours before batting practice encouraged pranks and practical jokes that would often be considered in poor taste in polite society. Maybe the best example was Johnny Lindell, the good-natured, power-hitting, part-time left fielder for the New York Yankees. Lindell was a slow-moving and massive fellow who stood six feet four inches and towered over many of his teammates. He often was the clubhouse jokester whose humor involved his huge male member. Unsuspecting newspaper readers would suddenly find it flopping over the top of a page in the sports section or falling into the latest stock market reports. Card players remained constantly alert to Lindell's whereabouts in the clubhouse, because the swinging member might slap against someone's back or intrude into a convenient armpit. Vertically challenged players were Lindell's targets in post-game showers. He would stand behind Yankee shortstop Phil Rizzuto, who was five-feet seven if stretched on the rack, and rest his member on Rizzuto's shoulder, much to the latter's horror, as he yelled and jumped away while everyone laughed uproariously.

Such hi-jinks helped to break the boredom of the clubhouse atmosphere and to strengthen the camaraderie of the team. Autographing boxes of baseballs before a game, for instance, was a tedious chore avoided by some players whenever possible. The lengthy road trips created repetitive demands on the free time of players. When boxes of twelve or more baseballs appeared for their signature, players scattered to take care of suddenly more important tasks and to put off signing as long as possible. One day before a game I was making a list of things to do when Bob Feller looked over my shoulder and said, "Hey Kid! You've got good handwriting. Can you do my name on a ball?" Me? Become Bob Feller's substitute?! I was speechless. He must have thought the visitor's clubhouse hired mutes. Feller, in his prime, was the fastest pitcher of his era and threw three no-hit games. Using a high leg-kick and unique pivot, he delivered an explosive fast ball and a terrifying fast-breaking curve with effective wildness. In 1948, he claimed his seventh strike-out crown, while winning 19 games after a slow start. Most fans didn't know, and the press never mentioned that Feller had occasional muscular twitching of the left side of his face. The sudden, repeated distortion between mouth and eye might have interrupted conversations, I thought, and also must have given a humorous twist to taking signals from the catcher as he faced the batter. My answer to his request was delayed even longer as these images refused to leave and others arrived.

His total income, including post-season exhibition or "barnstorming" games, had reached $150,000 causing him to incorporate himself as Bo-Fel, Inc. From then on teammates called him "Inky," (short for incorporated). Did he want me to write "Inky Feller", or "Bob Feller", on baseballs, I wondered? But "Bob" it was to be, and from then on I became "Bob Feller" on dozens of boxes of balls. When other Cleveland Indian players discovered his scheme, I was given even more work in my spare time. I also became "Lou Boudreau" who was over-burdened with managerial responsibilities while still a player, and who was pleased to find a surrogate for the ball-signing task. I offered to help him make out the batting order for games, but he declined. It was 1948, and Cleveland was en route to a world championship during the first season of my three-year dream experience.

Signing a baseball was not a casual act for some players, typically those who were considered "stars." These players had their own part of the ball's surface for their signature, not the name of a player of lesser status. If a baseball or a box of baseballs arrived at a player's locker for signatures and his spot on the ball of every ball in the box already was used, a petulant refusal to sign could result. Enter Danny the batboy and his ability to duplicate the signatures of some of his heroes.

Known as "Inky" to his teammates and "Rapid Robert" to his fans.

BOB FELLER

I soon learned the favorite spots on the ball for Bob Feller, Lou Boudreau, Joe DiMaggio, Larry Berra, and Ted Williams. Bob Feller (or Danny) always signed in the upper-most part of the widest area between the stitches where Ted Williams also could be found. Lou Boudreau (or Danny), Joe DiMaggio, and Larry Berra wanted the narrow space between the stitches. Johnny Orlando, the Boston Red Sox traveling clubhouse man and part-time trainer, acted as a buffer against requests for Williams's time and signatures and gave me the signal to approach when Williams was ready to scribble quickly on the horsehide.

Ballplayers in the late forties and early fifties didn't sell their signatures on balls, scorecards, and other convenient surfaces. Moreover, autographs then were more legible than the hasty scrawls of today's athletes whose handwriting resembles a secret code. Today our heroes tend to save their best and clearest signings for cash sale, yet another example, in my opinion, of baseball's surrender to greed and a careless disregard of those who idolize the game and its players. Commerce now reigns.

Not all clubhouse behavior that I witnessed would be amusing, because the color barrier was being breached in the major leagues. Resentment of black players was deep and openly expressed on and off the field. White players frequently could be heard to say, "We don't need no niggers on this team takin' a white man's spot on the roster." Some teams were reluctant even to consider talented black players. This was especially true in Detroit, Boston, and New York. The latter two ball clubs had opportunities to bring Willy Mays up to the major leagues from Negro baseball, but held back for reasons of race. Only a few years before, games had been cancelled in Georgia and Florida to prevent black players from being on the same diamond as white men. Ballparks in the South conformed with Jim Crow laws and had segregated bleacher and grandstand sections, plus toilet facilities and drinking fountains labeled "Colored", much longer than history books admit.

In July 1947 Bill Veeck brought Larry Doby to the Cleveland Indians where he would begin a series of seven All-Star appearances and play center field for the world champions in 1948. Yet he and other black players were denied entry to hotels and restaurants. In Detroit, visiting teams stayed downtown at the Book Cadillac or Statler Hotels, the city's finest. Black players stayed and took their meals elsewhere. Opposing teams were hostile to Doby's presence on the field and spat on him during games. White fans in the grandstand at Briggs Stadium had a steady supply of racial slurs and obscenities ready for his every move. During the late 1940s, black fans usually sat in the bleachers in Detroit and would provide the only applause for him.

The clubhouse did not provide a welcome refuge for Doby either, as other players failed to speak or interact with him. He was seldom included in clubhouse post-game conversation. I never saw any real attempt to make him feel part of the team. Teammates largely ignored him and his contribution to the Indians's success. I often

Racial insults didn't prevent him from being an All-Star

LARRY DOBY

was stunned by the isolation imposed by the players, except for Al Rosen, Cleveland's Jewish third baseman. Even though Detroit was a segregated city with an ample number of bigots, I wasn't prepared to see a person treated this way because I was a minority in a black high school with an absence of racial tension. Fond memories decades later of many pleasant experiences at Briggs Stadium would be interrupted by images of such distasteful behavior toward people of another race.

Regardless of what went on in the clubhouse among the players, I still had many chores to do each day. I was once re-mopping the clubhouse floor after a game when my first efforts did not please Fat Frank. He had said, "You call that a clean floor? I know amputees who could do a better job. Don't forget to do the shithouse. It's your turn." Compliments were not often given to batboys for fear of spoiling them. If you wanted compliments, home was the best place to get them. The clubhouse had to be cleaned, baseball shoes shined, uniforms prepared for the following day; all work had to be finished before going home. No time the next day, if school was still in session. I happened to be dragging the heavy wet mop past the locker of Jerry Coleman, rookie 2nd baseman for the Yankees in 1949 and San Diego Padre broadcaster for many years after he quit playing.

"Hey Kid! Can you help me with something?"

"Yessir, Mr. Coleman," I replied.

"Can you wash these socks for me by tomorrow's game?" he asked.

I looked into his locker and saw that his personal items box was overflowing with soiled and smelly sanitary socks, the hose worn under the stirrup black uniform socks of the Yankees. Apparently the pile of socks represented weeks of accumulation during a long journey with Detroit as its end-point. Before I could reconsider my quick response, I remembered what Fat Frank had pounded into the batboys day after day, "this is the best visitor's clubhouse in the American League. Don't fuck up."

"You'll have them tomorrow," I said, thinking that homework for school the following day was cancelled. I probably would have to wing it in Spanish class, because there wouldn't be time to study when I went home.

The clubhouse lacked a washing machine which meant several hours of hand washing in the sink lay ahead of me after other chores were finished, such as putting sweaty jockstraps and sweat shirts into the dryer and cleaning the toilets and showers. At 10:30 that night Coleman's socks were clean, and I caught the streetcar for home, hoping that there would be leftovers from supper, before falling asleep conjugating Spanish verbs in the subjunctive. The next day when Coleman arrived in the clubhouse, all of the sanitary socks that he possessed were arranged neatly in his locker, ready for use, even the ones with holes. I never found out whether I had successfully upheld the reputation of "the best visitor's clubhouse in the American League." Perhaps he was too worried about keeping

A real war hero with the medals to prove it

JERRY COLEMAN

his starting role as a rookie, or treating an ulcer, to thank the kid who worked for his heroes for $3.00 a day.

One day before a game near the end of the season, several Yankee ballplayers gathered in the trainer's room to be taped and to have pitching arms massaged. Conversation turned to plans after season's end. A favorite pastime among the men with a strong rural background was hunting for a variety of game at different locations across the South.

First Yankee: "Didja ever shoot in the Ozarks?"

Second Yankee: "No, but I'm fixin' to this Fall."

Third Yankee: "Well, last time I tried the woods along the White River, I got me the damndest cyst you ever saw."

About that time, Larry Berra, later to gain boundless notoriety as "Yogi," strolled by the trainer's room and overheard his teammates talking. He looked puzzled and remarked, "Geez, guys, what kind of a bird is a cyst?" Such an opportunity was not to be missed to gleefully lead Yogi into the wilderness.

The third Yankee responded, "You never seen no cyst? It's got long, white, tail feathers and a blue belly, and flies backward so goddamned fast, when it came out of the brush, I almost dropped my gun the first time I seen it. But the next one I seen, I unloaded both barrels. There's feathers and bird shit everywhere."

"Are you kiddin'," Yogi said. "I want to go with ya, if ya go this year." With this response from Berra, the group could no longer contain itself and began to laugh loudly at their teammate's expense.

Berra was not always the target of such well-intentioned humor. Once he even topped his teammates in a discussion involving sexual prowess and unusual sexual acts. With his teammates attempting to reach new heights of exaggeration about favorite positions for sex and the cleverness of their wives and/or girlfriends in pleasing them, Yogi interjected, "Aw geez, dat's nothin'. Did ya ever do it in a bathtub full of Jello? Once when I got home after a game, my wife called me upstairs and said she had a surprise for me." All present nodded in agreement that this was an exciting woman and that Yogi indeed was a lucky man. For more than fifty years, I often wondered, what flavor of Jello?

Earlier I referred to Berra's first name rather than as Yogi, for in the period of my service to the visiting teams, he usually was called Larry and autographed baseballs as such. When I was asked to get signatures of the Yankee players for boxes of baseballs, I started with Bobby Brown at the first locker near the clubhouse entrance, because he and Berra understood my assignment and their responsibility to help me, time permitting. I noticed medical textbooks in Brown's locker, for he would one day become a successful physician and eventually president of the American League. Berra, in the next locker, kept a steady supply of comic books in order to keep up with the adventures of his favorite mythical heroes. I worked

He signed baseballs and other autographs as Larry Berra at this time.

YOGI BERRA

my way down the row of lockers past those of Joe Di Maggio, Charlie Silvera, and "Major" Ralph Houk before reaching the tunnel that led to the dugout. It was impossible to get signatures from all of the players for a box of baseballs in one day, because I usually had so many other responsibilities.

Access to the visitor's dugout from the tunnel leading to the clubhouse required a three-step climb after passing the urinal that was cleaned at least once every ten years. The shorter portion of the padded dugout bench was located to the right of the steps. The end wall held a telephone box that served as connection to the bullpen, out of sight, in deep center field beyond the flagpole. A rack with multiple openings to hold bats for the game occupied the other end of the dugout with a drinking fountain. Batboys were expected to carry, not drag, the heavy canvas bag filled with bats from the clubhouse along the tunnel and into the dugout before batting practice. Some players preferred to be responsible for their own bats and to rack them before game time. Each player's number was placed on the bat's knob end for quick identification.

It was the batboy's job during a game not only to replace a bat in its bat rack slot after a hitter's turn at bat, but to know when to take a bat or combination of bats to the on-deck circle for the next hitter. Some players wanted to carry two or three regular bats to the circle, swinging them there in order to loosen up for their turn at the plate. Others liked to swing a heavy leaded bat instead of game bats. Some players wanted a clean towel on which to kneel while waiting to hit. This was the preference of Johnny Pesky, Red Sox third baseman in the late forties. I was waiting in the on-deck circle, holding the heavy bat, and kneeling next to a clean towel when center fielder Dominic DiMaggio ("The Little Professor" or "The Little Dago") led off the game. Pesky soon joined me, knelt on the clean towel, took the heavy bat from me and exclaimed softly, "Danny, you're a good man, but you shit too close to the house." Taken by surprise, I laughed loudly, much to the displeasure of the home plate umpire who had just called a strike on DiMaggio. They both glared at me, but for different reasons; lack of respect for the umpire and disruption of the batter's concentration. Pesky came to my aid, by saying, "Don't blame the kid, I made him laugh."

DiMaggio walked, and Pesky slashed a sharp single to left. I racked their bats in the dugout and waited there until Ted Williams finished swinging several bats as he stood in the on-deck circle and then stepped confidently to the plate. I quickly retrieved Williams's bat as he ran to first after drawing a walk, and I returned to the dugout to help Junior Stephens, shortstop and clean-up hitter.

If a batboy did his job well, people in the grandstand seldom paid any attention except when he returned to the dugout with a relief pitcher's warm-up jacket. Sounds simple, yet the act was fraught with potential for massive embarrassment. A Briggs Stadium tradition involved home team and visiting team bat boys running from their dugouts to second base, arriving there at the same time as the relief pitcher coming from the center field bull pens, then taking their warm-up jackets on the run and returning to the dugouts by the time the new pitcher reached the mound.

Consider for a moment the pressure on a teenaged batboy in front of 40 or 50 thousand people to correctly time departure from the dugout so as not to noticeably slow down en route to second base and to get back to the dugout before the new pitcher climbed the mound. It was considered very bad form to wait at second base for the incoming pitcher. If the journey was done well and in rhythm, appreciative fans would provide enthusiastic applause for the boy's journey. Once again, Briggs Stadium showed why it was the best run stadium in the major leagues. High-quality performance, even by batboys for a minute or so, demanded pre-game preparation while players took batting practice before the game. Batboys ran rehearsal laps from dugout to second base to dugout to loosen up, especially in cool weather. On rainy days, with treacherous footing, spikes always were checked for clots of mud before leaving the dugout on the run. No stumbling, or hamstring pulls were allowed. Batboys didn't want sympathy for an injury, they wanted applause from the thousands present. Imagine the feeling when the noise is for your efforts.

My exploits on the field at Briggs Stadium actually made history in the spring of 1949. I arrived at the clubhouse one morning when Fat Frank greeted me as he wolfed down a Danish with his coffee, "Do you got a glove and spikes? You play ball doncha, when there are no home games?"

"Whenever I can," I replied.

"You don't throw like no sissy, right?" he questioned. "Well, we have to know for sure anyway; let's go out to the field."

My curiosity was aroused, yet I didn't completely trust Fat Frank's motives. I remembered him sending the Japanese clubhouse boy, Masi Sakow, to find a left-handed monkey wrench in the maintenance storeroom, an errand dutifully carried out by the diffident Masi. Another time when things were slow in the work schedule, Masi scurried off in search of a banana seeder because he was told, "we can't give no bananas with seeds to DiMaggio for his pre-game snack. He hates them and he expects the best from us." Hilarity accompanied each of the foolish errands, for Masi's mastery of English was far from perfect, and he was maximum naive. Therefore my antennae sensed the possibility of a practical joke at my expense, as I walked out to the dugout with Fat Frank. We left the clubhouse at the same time, but Fat Frank arrived much later while his girth moved from side to side with each step forward. I fully expected that he would collapse on the dugout steps, threes steps upward and a huge gasp for air by him at each step. "You and Russ (another batboy) play catch and increase your distance between throws," Fat Frank directed. We tossed the ball back and forth while standing about 50 to 60 feet apart in foul territory. Then I increased the distance to 90 feet, then to 120, and farther into right field foul territory. Luckily my arm was strong and accurate. My return throws now were intentionally on one hop to my partner.

Fat Frank yelled that I should stop at about 250 to 275 feet from home plate. I threw easily back toward the dugout, bouncing the ball so that it could be fielded cleanly by Russ, who then changed his position to be closer to the backstop. Finally I was sending the ball to the correct spot, which was the reason for the exercise. My audition was not an elaborate practical joke, but preparation for retrieving foul balls during a game. Fans had been climbing over the low wall in right field, emboldened by alcohol, to grab a souvenir from the playing field. And so, to the best of my knowledge, I became the first ballboy of this kind in the American League, sitting on my short-legged black and white stool and waiting for ground balls or line drives not hit into the grandstand. I fielded each ball and returned it with a long throw back to the visitor's dugout or near the backstop where another batboy supplied the home plate umpire with new baseballs. I never made an error when assigned to right field. The only time in three seasons that I received a "well-done" after the game from Fat Frank was when he had heard Harry Heilemann, then calling the game on radio, compliment me on catching a hard hit ball off the bat of Tiger outfielder Vic Wertz.

Chapter 3

Do I Gotta Learn Another Language?

"I admire him now much more than ever before. He
showed so much courage as he lay there on the floor.
The way he looked up at me and kept smiling."
Ruth Steinhagen, the day after she shot Eddie Waitkus
St. Louis Post-Dispatch, June 16, 1949

My earliest years were spent in a very small community in southernillinois (that's one word in the local dialect) where I learned to read by careful study of the sports section in the St. Louis Post-Dispatch. The Cardinals were my baseball team of choice, and radios were turned to station KMOX so that we could follow the daily achievements of the Cooper brothers (Mort and Walker), Stan "the Man" Musial, Whitey Kurowski, and Marty "Slatts" Marion. Verbal communication in such a rural setting used many colorful, and, to the outsider, almost incomprehensible expressions. If you felt hungry, you felt lank. You could be so hungry your stomach would think your throat was cut. People went uptown to shop, because the town square was at a higher elevation than much of the community. Eating too many pieces of cucumber or slices of watermelon could cause a severe case of gas on the stomach, locally described as "being blowed up like a toad."

I carried these expressions with me for the rest of my life and into Detroit's inner city where the stage of adolescence was waiting. There I quickly adopted the language of the streets in neighborhoods with rapidly changing populations of blacks and southern hill people who were arriving in Detroit to find jobs during the booming 1940s. Throughout my years in Detroit public schools, I was part of a white Protestant minority, a situation that gave me valuable insights into the viewpoints of others. I easily acquired the argot of Jewish and black friends as I added two more languages to my collection.

In April of 1948, I began to learn a fourth language, that of major league baseball, it's common expressions, terminology, and players' nicknames. Baseball players long have been identified by nicknames—some humorous, some odd, some politically incorrect in our society today. They were likely to be names given to ballplayers by each other, not by journalists or by radio broadcasters of the era. Certain nicknames need brief explanation. All were typical of basic communication in the locker room and of male camaraderie on the playing field.

Tommy Byrne (NY), **The Broadcaster**, was notoriously wild, although an effective starting pitcher for the Yankees; he could be heard on the mound or in the dugout delivering a play-by-play account of even his game.

Dom DiMaggio (Bos.), **The Little Professor, The Little Dago**, smaller than his brother and wearing glasses, he had a scholarly appearance.

Joe DiMaggio (NY), **The Dago, The Yankee Clipper**, rude, ethnic reference to his Italian background; his quiet and effortless play likened to the movement of a great sailing ship.

Walt Dropo (Det.) **Moose**, his hometown (Moosup, Ct.), not his size, responsible for the moniker.

Walter Evers (Det.), **Hoot**, a big fan of cowboy file star Hoot Gibson; supposedly made a hooting noise as a baby and was given the nickname.

Ferris Fain (Phila.), **Burrhead**, descriptive of a bad haircut.

Bob Feller (Cleve), **Rapid Robert, Inky (Inc.)**, the media and the public knew him as "Rapid Robert," but to his teammates, he was "Inky" after he incorporated himself for business purposes as Bo-Fel, Inc.

Hank Greenberg (Det.), **Hammerin' Hank**, A big and powerful right-hand batter whose .92 runs batted in per game during his career was bested only by Lou Gehrig and Sam Crawford.

Tommy Henrich (NY), **Old Reliable**, with the game at stake in the ninth inning and a runner or runners on base, he was dependably deadly in the clutch.

Johnny Hopp (St. L. C/NY), **Hippity**, what else could it be.

Ralph Houk (NY), **The Major**, the rank he attained in the World War II Army service; eventually replaced Casey Stengel as Yankee manager in 1961.

Art Houtteman (Det.), **Hard-Luck**, survived car wreck to lose many games without team support at bat and in the field.

Freddie Hutchinson (Det.), **The Great Stoneface**, a candidate for Mt. Rushmore, prepackaged.

Charlie Keller (NY), **King Kong**, thick and hairy arms complemented a physiognomy and gait, which to some observers, immediately suggested relation to Hollywood's renowned ape.

Ellis Kinder (Bos.), **Old Folks**, arrived late in the big leagues.

Don Kolloway (Chi./Det.), **Cab**, play on words referring to the entertainer Cab Callaway.

Don Lenhardt (Bos./St. L./Det.), **Footsie**, a truly remarkable foundation.

Hubert Leonard (Wash.), **Dutch**, couldn't escape his ancestry.

Ed Lopat (Chi./NY), **Steady Eddie**, always a reliable, consistent performer in control on the mound; facing him could put batters into a slump for several games.

Connie Mack (Phil.), **Mr. Baseball, The Tall Tactician**, fifty years as manager; wore street clothes not uniform to manage; known for waving scorecard to position players on the field; 1948 his last first-division team.

Walter Masterson (Wash.), **Specs**, one of the few major league players to wear spectacles on the field, his tinted aviator shades would have been considered very cool decades later.

Don Mosse (Cleve.), **Ears**, why wasn't it Dumbo? He had the ears for it.

Hal Newhouser (Det.), **Turkey Neck, Prince Hal**, in the newspapers and on the radio, Newhouser was known as Prince Hal, but to ever-alert bench jockeys of rival teams, the movement of his neck and head as he walked suggested everyone's favorite Thanksgiving bird.

Frank Overmire (Det.), **Stubby**, vertically challenged lefty who complemented the T-N-T rotation.

Dave Philley (Chi., etc.), **Grumpy**, switch-hitting, pinch-hitter par excellance, (nine consecutive hits) in search of a smile.

Vic Raschi (NY), **Aunt Susie**, a curveball was sometimes referred to as Aunt Susie and Raschi had difficulty developing an effective one and preferred the "heater" or fastball instead.

Red Sox, **The Dead Sox**, common description of Boston's failed offense on long road trips away from Fenway Park.

Allie Reynolds (NY), **Super Chief**, Native-American ancestry; a commanding presence when he took the mound.

Phil Rizzuto (NY), **Scooter**, knew how to play hitters and position himself in the field where his glove and quick release of fielded balls led to description of scooting about at shortstop.

Saul Rogovin (Det.), **Sleepy**, he could sleep anywhere, any time; didn't know the meaning of "hyper".

Joe Schultz (St. L.B.), **Ol' Shitfuck**, undistinguished catcher who managed the Tigers (briefly) and the fledgling Seattle Pilots and was known for repeated use of this combination of nouns and verbs.

Casey Stengel (NY), **The Ol' Perfesser**, his version of English known as Stengelese; studied dentistry; tireless talker about baseball; best year managing probably 1949 when Yankees won pennant despite injury-plagued season.

George Sternweiss (NY), **Snuffy**, suffered from a lifelong sinus condition; American League batting champ in 1945 with third lowest average in league history—.309—winning it on the last day of the season.

George Tebbetts (Bos.), **Birdie**, not many people know his first name was George because he was such a chatterbox. His locker in the clubhouse was near that of Ted Williams ostensibly so that they could talk each other to death.

Earl Torgeson (Det.), **The Earl of Snohomish**, he was big in his hometown back in Washington state.

Paul Trout (Det.), **Dizzy**, nicknamed by local newspaper in the community where he played in the minor leagues; his erratic behavior drew fans to the ballpark.

Virgil Trucks (Det.), **Fire**, his blazing fastballs soon created the name; pitched two no-hitters in 1952.

Hal Wagner (Det.), **Monk**, he was an undistinguished catcher with the Tigers in 1948; his appearance and actions drew derisive characterization of possible simian ancestry.

Washington Senators, **The Griffmen**, reference to Clark Griffith, owner of the team.

Ted Williams (Bos.), **Splendid Splinter**, tall and slender in pre-WWII years, the last player to hit .400 for a season.

The "broadcaster" shown here in a role he relished, that of a pinch hitter.

TOMMY BRYNE

In the absence of an *Aunt Susie*, he had to rely on a good heater.

VIC RASCHI

In the dugout and on the field, a variety of highly colorful expressions were used to describe images and events and to characterize the participants in games. Complete membership in diamond society required not only exhaustive knowledge of current expressions, but the ability to create new ones as the occasion demanded. A talented and effective bench jockey could, whenever needed, immediately come up with richly-textured language implying sexual promiscuity by female relatives or another player's supposedly hidden perversions—perhaps involving animals. The most graphic comments must remain untold although other items may be appreciated in the following list.

1. **Arlie Latham**—a futile attempt by an infielder to field a ground ball

2. **atom ball**—a batted ball hit directly at a fielder

3. **Aunt Susie**—a curve ball

4. **Baltimore chop**—a batted ball hitting the ground close to home plate, then bouncing upward high enough for the batter to be safe

5. **barber(ing)**—a talkative player; persistent facial stubble; to throw close to the batter's head

6. **blind staggers**—awkward maneuvering in order to catch a high wind-blown fly ball

7. **bow tie**—a Satchel Paige pitch at the batter's throat

8. **bush**—unprofessional conduct by anyone

9. **chaw**—chewing tobacco; essential for the macho player

10. **Chinese line drive**—a pop fly

11. **climb the ladder**—consecutively higher and higher pitches to make the batter swing at one out of the strike zone

12. **cripple hitter**—a batter who hits when well behind in the count or who hits a "mistake" pitch by the pitcher

13. **dugoutese**—slang used by a limited group of ballplayers

14. **fight off**—persistent fouling off of pitches until the batter gets the one he wants, e.g. Luke Appling

15. **frozen rope**—a very hard hit ball, straight and parallel to the ground

16. **Hey kid!**—used by ballplayers to call a batboy for a task or errand; a greeting given to batboys by ballplayers

17. **hitch**—a hesitation, extra motion, or other quirk affecting a batter's timing and preventing a smooth swing

18. **hole in his swing**—a batter's area of weakness or vulnerable spot in the swinging arc made by the bat

19. **humpbacked liner**—a line drive that sinks quickly; a cross between a "frozen rope" and a "parachute"

20. **kitchen**—the high, inside part of the strike zone, (cheese for your kitchen) e.g. Vic Raschi

21. **meat**—a baseball player; a common friendly greeting used among players

22. **muff**—to drop a grounder or a fly ball; to miss a catch or to screw up a play

23. **off the schneid**—a team or a hitter coming out of a slump

24. **one o'clock hitter**—player who hits well in batting practice and poorly during a game at 3:00 or 3:30 p.m.

25. **one ol' cat**—one base, a player at the plate, a pitcher, and one or more fielders; run to base and back before being put out

26. **pea**—a pitched or a batted ball moving so fast it seems smaller than it is; a pitcher was encouraged by his teammates to "hum that pea"

27. **pick**—to successfully field a ground ball, especially one difficult to handle

28. **picket line**—the three outfielders who can "picket" or skillfully field balls hit to them in the air and on the ground

29. **punchout**—a strikeout

30. **rabbit ears**—an overly sensitive player or umpire especially ready to hear and respond to comments and taunts of bench jockeys and fans in the stands

31. **red ass,**—a tough, angry player; a fire-brand; a player who is easily riled

32. **rhubarb**—a ruckus with the umpire; confusion; a fight between players or between players and fans

33. **riffle**—a hardy swing at a pitched ball

34. **rubbing mud**—a mildly abrasive soil smeared on baseballs by the umpire before a game to remove gloss or shine in order to permit an easier grip of the ball by pitchers (introduced to the American League in the late 1930s by Connie Mack and into the National League in the 1950s)

35. **sanitaries**—long, white socks worn underneath stirrup uniform socks

36. **scatter arm**—a pitcher or a fielder susceptible to wild pitches and throwing errors

37. **shieny**—a highly derogatory term for a Jewish player

38. **soupbone**—a pitcher's throwing arm but sometimes the throwing arm of any player

39. **"stick it in his ear"**—nasty advice by a bench jockey for his pitcher to hit the batter in the head

40. **that one'll bring rain**—a very high fly ball

41. **up the chute, up the shaft**—any ball hit straight up over home plate

42. **Venus de Milo outfield**—an outfield lacking strong, accurate throwing-arms

One expression which had special meaning for Danny the Batboy was that of Baseball Annie. This was applied to unattached women who wanted the company and affection of baseball players, or anyone else in a baseball uniform. Later, during the age of rock music, such camp followers would be labeled "groupies." Baseball Annies made their availability known at the ballpark and at the hotel where teams stayed on the road. At the ballpark, even batboys attracted young female fans who suggested sexual favors in exchange for game tickets, autographed balls, or any paraphernalia carrying a team logo. An eager young Annie enthusiastically called to Danny in the dugout while he packed up bats after a game, "Can you get me two tickets for the Yankee series? I'll do anything you want the whole weekend!"—she clearly overestimated Danny's influence with the Briggs Stadium ticket office.

On June 15, 1949, Philadelphia Phillies first baseman, Eddie Waitkus, was shot by Baseball Annie, Ruth Steinhagen, in her hotel room and survived to play the next season. The near-tragic event obviously monopolized clubhouse conversation the next day as well as most of the banter around the batting cage during batting practice. One of the players offered Danny some fatherly advice, "Let that be a lesson to ya, kid. That's what happens when you can't get it up. So be sure to get plenty of sleep and go heavy on the protein—steak and eggs—if you don't want to catch three slugs in the chest." Needless to say, the players did not feel terrorized by overly aggressive women fans.

Batting practice prior to an important game or the beginning of a three-game series with the Yankees, Indians, or Red Sox, or a Friday night game provided the opportunity for players to engage in one of their favorite pastimes, "shooting the beaver." Initially intended as an overview of the gathering fans to guess final attendance for the game, one player and then another would locate attractive women in the grandstand, especially behind the visitor's dugout. Brief comments, or at

He would have preferred a more civil introduction to Ruth Steinhagen.

EDDIE WAITKUS

times notes, were passed to responsive female fans who wanted to be noticed by the players. Long road trips away from home required creativity in developing post-game social activities, some of which had unintended consequences. A well-known veteran outfielder was heard to reply, when asked what he thought was the greatest challenge he had faced in the major leagues, "Trying to explain to my wife why she had to take penicillin for my root canal."

If you were lucky, you got to go onto the field for batting practice before the game. All but one of the boys remained in the clubhouse doing chores and running errands right up to game time. There always were last minute things to do for someone, maybe a roast beef sandwich from Hoot Robinson's restaurant for Fat Frank. People assumed that batboys, visiting team and home team, were a tight-knit, friendly group, but this was not the case. Little warmth of friendship passed among our band of boys in the visitor's clubhouse. We came to work, did our jobs, helping one another if needed, and went home dead tired. Some explanation of the lack of expected camaraderie, at least from my viewpoint, lay in Detroit's geography. The city was sharply cut into two distinct and opposing sections by Woodward Avenue.

Deep and senseless rivalry between the East side and the West side could reach its extreme with the click of a switchblade knife. I happened to be the only kid in the clubhouse group from the West side, and this was reflected in the attitudes of the other boys toward me, sometimes in subtle ways—forgotten messages, Fat Frank's instructions delayed, or a player's false request. We went our separate ways after games and only joined for common purpose to make the visitor's clubhouse best in the American League. Boys working in the visitor's clubhouse normally weren't invited to socialize with the kids assigned to the Tiger clubhouse. Did the latter think they were better because they wore the white home uniforms with the Detroit "D", and we wore the traveling grey road uniforms? We were teenagers. Judge for yourself.

Entering the ballpark for work each day was like going into an oasis; the rhythm of activities and the people inside were excluded from the reality of the outside world by the square block of thick walls facing the four surrounding neighborhood streets. Once inside sights, tastes, and smells fused with stadium sounds to create personality of place elsewhere unmatched. The clatter of cleaning carts and the chatter of sweepers and concession workers echoed around the interior of the lower deck grandstand.

A small army of sweepers and refuse collectors exchanged challenges and insults as they hurried to finish the day's tasks. The aroma of stale beer and yesterday's cigarette and cigar smoke lingered in the air under the grandstand. Half-eaten hot dog buns stuck to the concrete floor with mustard and onions and fought for space with crushed "coffin nails" and "Cubans." Restrooms reeked of beer mixed with urine. I didn't envy the cleanup crews who were paid a lot more than I was. I gladly would have done my job for nothing, but not those unfortunate guys who needed even a dirty job.

As game time approached the smell of fresh hot dogs on grills in concessions stands smothered the unpleasant odors of the previous day except in the rest rooms. The ballpark menus didn't have the diversity of future decades. No pizza, barbeque, or strawberry shortcake which would appear later to accompany peanuts, potato chips, and ice cream bars or cotton candy. Sweepers were hard pressed to remove all of the refuse from the previous day. Teams of workers moved row by row in the grandstand, in lower and upper decks, removing all of the trash and putting seats against their backs ready for the next game. Out on the field more skilled workers carefully prepared the playing surface for the Bengals and their visitors. The infield was manicured, mowed, and swept while outfield sprinklers applied water between the foul lines after mowing was completed. In the late forties and early fifties, segregation prevailed, when possible, according to assignments. Black or black and white teams labored in and under the grandstand, and all-white crews prepared the playing field.

Spectators arriving for the game didn't resemble fans in the late twentieth and early twenty-first centuries. As players and batboys watched people find their seats, they saw men wearing hats and occasionally suits and ties, except on the hottest days, and women with dresses, hats and matching shoes. Fans today would expect a formal ceremony rather than a sporting event given the appearance of those in attendance. During summer men usually sported straw hats, soft or stiff, which would be thrown onto to the field on Labor Day because, regardless of temperature, the date signaled summer's end.

Chapter 4

Where's My Chaw?

"Sometimes when I walk down the street, I bet people
will say, there goes Roy Hobbs, the best there ever was
in the game"—from the movie *The Natural.*

The visitor's clubhouse at Briggs Stadium was connected to the dugout and playing field by a long cement-walled tunnel whose entire length of floor was covered by a boardwalk. A common part of pre-game preparation by ball players was creating a chaw of leaf chewing tobacco. Not everyone wanted the same brand of tobacco for their chaw. Some opted for "Mail Pouch," some for "Red Man", others for "Dat's da Stuff," all well-known in the South among men who needed to deform their faces with a lump of wadded leaf in their cheeks. A drive through the South in the late 1940s and early 1950s still revealed these brand names in fading letters on roofs and sides of barns. Chewing tobacco was as much a part of baseball as balls and strikes, fair and foul.

It was not just a simple wad of leaf; admixture of peppermint or spearmint flavored snuff completed the process at times. Chaws were inserted in the clubhouse, bats were selected for batting practice, spikes to be broken in were tied securely, and new gloves were tucked under one arm as players walked down the tunnel to the dugout. Batting and infield practice occupied the team for approximately the next hour and a half. Players then returned quickly to the clubhouse, often passing through the tunnel at a gallop. Chaws were removed on the run and stuck to the concrete sides of the tunnel willy-nilly. Sweaty undershirts and uniforms were quickly changed, game shoes selected, and lucky charms were donned prior to game's start. If a player was in the midst of a hitting streak, however, sanitary socks might go unchanged for days or dirty uniforms would reappear until streaks-end. Players went unshaven for fear of breaking the spell. A few extremists refused to shower, in order not to break their run of good fortune. They soon were advised by caring teammates to make personal hygiene a greater priority. Eventually, the team surged back through the tunnel and players grabbed a chaw from the wall. Was it theirs? I was never convinced that owner and chaw had been reunited. Play Ball!! Finally, I would see my heroes in action as they hit, played defense, and pitched for the American League's eight teams.

Once in the dugout, another three steps were needed to reach the finely manicured playing surface, whose quality of maintenance set the standard for the rest of the American League. Industrialist owner, Walter O. Briggs, was the ultimate baseball fan and wanted to give the city of Detroit the best team in the best ballpark. The grounds crew and even the grandstand cleanup squads took pride in making the stadium the best place to play and the best place to watch a game in the late 40s and early 50s. Everyone who worked at the stadium adopted a work ethic to achieve these goals.

The playing surface also received loving care from a proud group of hard-working, cigar-chewing white men sporting an occasional beer belly as badge of after-game recreation and celebration. No blemish on the field went unnoticed as the outfield grass was mowed to resemble a smooth green carpet, and the dirt portion of the infield was raked constantly to remove clods of dirt that might cause bad hops for infielders. Grass in the infield was allowed to grow higher and thicker than in the outfield, in order to reduce the speed of ground balls and accommodate slow-footed Tiger players. The home plate area always was soaked with water to prevent rapid departure from the batter's box. Surfaces carrying foul lines at the infield margins were slanted downward away from the playing field to encourage bunted balls to roll into foul territory. Moreover, the number of games rained out was held to a minimum by the speed of the grounds crew in pulling the tarp over the infield. Even this menial task was held to a high standard of performance. Unrolling the heavy tarp and covering the infield was done on the run and in such a short time that appreciative fans gave the men a hardy round of applause for their effort. The response by fans for a job well-done was as much a part of Briggs Stadium's atmosphere as the intoxicating smell of ballpark hotdogs or the cry of the beer vendor in the stands:

"Your beer man's here!"

"Get your beer here!"

"Goebbel beer(Tigers radio sponsor) and E & B beer here!"

"Ice cold beer here!"

This informative call to the fans in the grandstand seats remains today as fresh as the time I first heard it, when my father first took me to a major league game. Ticket prices, however, were much cheaper then—five dollars at most for a good box seat. Usually we preferred seats higher above the box seat level in order to have a better view of the playing field. Lower deck box seats actually put some spectators at a viewing disadvantage. On the third base side of the field, for example, the second baseman and the first baseman were visible only above the waist or chest depending upon the position of the box seat because the field sloped upward from the lowest box seat level to make drainage of the field easier. Even a seat in the upper deck was not far from the field. Briggs Stadium, as did many ballparks in the era, except Cleveland's cavernous Municipal Stadium, brought fans close to the scene of the action. Only seats in the bleachers, 440 feet from home plate, and in the far reaches of the upper deck grandstand, did not share the intimacy of the best ball park in the American League.

For many hitters Briggs Stadium literally was a paradise with green seats and green walls providing an excellent background against which the flight of a pitched ball could be clearly seen. A two-deck grandstand wrapped all the way around to the center field upper-deck bleachers making Briggs Stadium the first complete two-deck ballpark in the major leagues. One of the most appealing features of the stadium was the nearness of its seats to the playing field. Fans had a sense of being close to the action, something that would be lost in the ballparks built in later decades. Like many of its contemporary structures, the stadium was designed so that the playing area would fit into a city block. Idiosyncrasies of shape were a matter of function not design. Foul poles in left and right field were 340 feet and 325 feet, respectively, from home plate. Power alleys at Briggs Stadium were 365 in left field and 370 feet in right field. Straight away center field measured an amazing 440 feet. Other long distances were 415 feet near the visitor's bullpen and 400 feet close to the Tiger bullpen gate. An especially curious feature of the playing space was the right field upper-deck overhang of ten feet at the foul pole, making a "short porch" of just 315 feet, exactly the distance of Boston's "Green Monster Wall" at Fenway Park. Ted Williams loved to hit in Briggs Stadium and often was overheard to say, "I'd play for nothing if I could be here for all my home games. I'd tattoo that goddamned short porch like Junior (Stephens) and Bobby (Doerr)(both right-handed batters) do at home."

Lighting for night games arrived late at Michigan and Trumbull Avenues. Following the 1947 season, 11 towers were installed with 1,458 lights that provided Detroit with the best lighting system in baseball. On June 15, 1948, Briggs Stadium was bathed by the floodlights as the 54,480 standing room crowd cheered Hal Newhouser as he beat the Philadelphia Athletics 4 to 1. That evening was one of many unforgettable experiences for a teenaged batboy.

Recreational baseball in the alleys and on the playgrounds of inner-city Detroit required only basic skills of throwing, batting, and fielding with little attention to the intricacies of the game. So I arrived at Briggs Stadium to work as batboy in the "bigs" with a huge amount of enthusiasm and little understanding of how the game really was played. The visitor's dugout was a front row seat, not only to observe the game, but to acquire valuable insights into its complex nature. There's an old saying that states, "you can't learn with your mouth open." In other words, be quiet and listen, which is exactly what a batboy does in the dugout until he hears—Hey Kid!—. After three years of watching seven visiting teams, I clearly understood the old baseball maxim, solid defense "up the middle" was the key to winning baseball. The shortstop, the second baseman and the center fielder usually handled at least 40% of the balls in play. Consider the middle defense plus catching position for the most successful teams in the late 40s and early 50s. The Yankees: Joe DiMaggio, Phil Rizzuto, Jerry Coleman, and Larry Berra (or Charlie Silvera); The Indians: Larry Doby, Lou Boudreau, Joe Gordon, and Jim Hegan; The Red Sox: Dom DiMaggio, Junior Stephens, Bobby Doerr, and Birdie Tebbetts. With this array of talent, these teams were guaranteed spots in the pennant race. If the key to generating offense was to put more runners on base, then well-executed defense decreased hits, lowered errors, and raised the probability of double plays.

During games, watch the movements of the keystone duo. Does the shortstop put his glove behind his back before the pitch? He's probably signaling the center and left fielders to be ready for a certain kind of pitch. Watch the second baseman and shortstop hold gloves in front of their faces before the pitch. They are hiding an open or closed mouth to indicate responsibility for covering the bag on an attempted steal. Johnny Pesky, Red Sox third baseman, once said to me, "Danny, a lot of good defense is anticipation, but you have to know what the pitcher intends to do on each pitch."

I began to realize that, before each pitch, the defensive players arranged themselves according to a sequence of priorities: starting with the kind of pitch to be thrown, followed by the nature of the game situation, and finally, the identity of the hitter and his tendencies. As an adult, years later, I emphasized good defensive play to Little League players old enough to appreciate the need to rearrange the playing field space according to frequently changing game situations. The wisdom gathered around the batting cage before major league games and in the dugout during games made me a better coach for the boys and, I hope, enhanced their enjoyment of baseball. The boys seldom were tense before an important game because, I like to think, they were imitating my heroes and following the collective advice of the DiMaggio brothers, Boudreau, and Doerr, who excelled by seeing baseball as a game involving relaxation, conditioned reflex, and mental alertness.

Reading the *Sporting News* every week enabled me to be up-to-date with batting averages and other players' stats when each visiting team arrived. The second half of the 1940s was a particularly exciting time to experience major league baseball up close and from the inside. After the Tigers victory over the Cubs in the 1945 World Series, Boston, New York, and Cleveland each won the World Title before the Yankees repeated in 1949 and edged the Red Sox before taking the World Series from the Brooklyn Dodgers. New players became stars, many returnees from military service began to approach the end of their careers, and some future Hall of Fame members continued to achieve greatness.

I followed the progress of players such as Luke Appling, Hank Majeski, Kenny Keltner, and Joe Page. The first two labored for the White Sox and the Athletics, the other two starred for the Indians and the Yankees, respectively. In a twenty-year career at shortstop with excellent range, Appling would retire after the 1950 season with a batting average of .310. He was a notorious complainer about minor and imagined ills, yet the more old 'Aches and Pains' complained, the better he played. Appling's batting skills, good speed, and ability to draw walks made him an excellent lead-off hitter. In 1936, his .388 average made him the first American League shortstop to win a batting title.

By far the most entertaining feature of Appling's play was his uncanny ability to foul off pitches, eventually drawing a walk or getting his pitch to rip through the infield or line into the outfield. He once asked the penurious management of the White Sox for two baseballs to use as gifts, but was refused because baseballs, he was told, were too costly ($2.75) and the 'Pale Hose' were too poor. During his first turn at bat thereafter, he intentionally fouled off the first ten pitches, then walked over to the box seats where club officials were watching the game and said, "So far that amounts to $27.50". He never again begged for balls to use as gifts.

Hank (Heine) Majeski was maybe the best defensive third baseman in the American League during the 1940s. In 1948 he set a major league fielding record at his position by posting a .988 percentage. I watched his every move on the field because I was an aspiring third baseman. I had good range, quick feet, a strong arm, and a chest that didn't surrender to bad hops. Although Majeski didn't hit for a high average, he was reliable in the clutch and once connected for six doubles in a double-header. He could hit the curve ball far better than the batboy who saw him as model. I never could understand why he was shuffled from team to team, five in all, during his stay in the 'bigs'.

Still another fine third baseman of the era played for the Indians. Kenny Keltner had a career year in 1948 as I watched him, carried his bats, and asked for pointers on third base play. He stroked 31 homers that season to accompany 119 runs batted in while hitting .297. In the single game play-off with Boston to decide the American League championship, Keltner clubbed a three-run shot to put Cleveland into the World Series. But Keltner was accustomed to such heroics and the glare of publicity for he had made the plays to stop Joe DiMaggio's 56-game hitting streak in 1941. Such a feat by the Cleveland infielder reinforced my

A foul ball expert with aches and pains

LUKE APPLING

interest in learning about the defensive side of the game, when we were able to have an occasional pre-game chat.

All-Star performances were not limited to defense as I watched and worked for teams visiting Detroit in the late 40s and in 1950. Joe Page of the Yankees, Hal Newhouser of the Tigers, and Mel Parnell of the Red Sox were remarkably successful pitchers. For five years southpaw Parnell was one of baseball's dominant pitchers and in 1949 used his devastating curve ball to finish with a record of 25-7, a 2.77 earned run average, plus 27 complete games! How baseball would change. Fifty years later, starting pitchers would attempt to go 'deep into the game' by lasting until the seventh inning. The second of this trio of illustrious lefties was Newhouser, an All-Star for seven consecutive years while using an excellent slider in his role as mainstay of Detroit's pitching staff. Newhouser already had won back-to-back most valuable player awards in 1944 and 1945 and was the toast of the Motor City when I joined the Tiger family. Joe Page was instantly more impressive over a few innings late in the game than the other two hurlers. An overpowering fastball made "Leftie" the premier reliever of his time. In 1948 he appeared in 55 (56 the previous season) games, and the following year, in 60 games, while saving 27 games—a league high in 1949. Page would be identified as a 'closer' today, performing the role of Mariano Rivera. Unlike the closers of today, Page averaged two innings when he took the mound and shortened his career as a result.

The aforementioned trio were not the only players to make headlines, while I cleaned the clubhouse, carried bats, and chased balls on the field. Major League baseball during the post-war period was especially fortunate to have players on every American League team that made the headlines and were well-known to baseball fans. The following individuals were a select few whose achievements awed a young teenaged batboy, namely; Vern (Junior) Stephens, Satchel Paige, Gus Zernial, and Ferris Fain. Each of these players deserves the attention of fans who want to recapture baseball's past.

Maybe the most colorful player of the lot was Leroy 'Satchel' Paige, who joined the Indians during the 1948 season. He was the most celebrated player in the Negro Leagues and used his hesitation pitch and pin-point control to make a major contribution to Cleveland's efforts that year. The doubters of his abilities at a 40-something age soon discovered why Satchel had been a sensation in the Negro Leagues. The first day he entered the visitor's clubhouse in Detroit, he wore two-toned, wing-tip brown shoes, a brown double breasted suit, several gold necklaces, a cool white fedora and more rings than he had fingers. If his appearance suggested otherwise, Paige, nevertheless, was completely serious on the mound, winning six games and losing only one in 1948. Satchel Paige's simple humor and memorable sayings provided baseball fans with many smiles and chuckles as

Most valuable player in the American League for two consecutive years.

HAL NEWHOUSER

would Yogi Berra in future years. Several of Paige's quotable sayings, overheard in the clubhouse, were: "How old would you be if you didn't know how old you were?—"Age is a question of mind over matter. If you don't mind, it don't matter." Upon his induction into the Hall of Fame in 1971, he said, "The one change is that baseball has turned Paige from a second-class citizen into a second-class immortal." An observation of his that proved increasingly true over the years was: "all the young hitters today try to hit homeruns all the time. There's no more squeeze or drag bunting."

Bunting never occupied the thoughts of Vern (Junior) Stephens during Red Sox games. A perennial All-Star at shortstop, he and Ted Williams, in 1949, were one of the most awesome power-hitting duos in baseball history. Williams slugged 43 homeruns, Stephens 39, and each knocked in 159 runs. With Stephens batting cleanup behind Williams, Ted usually got better pitches to hit. One of my biggest thrills at Briggs Stadium was watching these two in action as they tattooed the outfield seats in right and left and the fences and walls of the power alleys.

Gus Zernial was another long-ball hitter who was just beginning his career in the '40s. Zernial may have left the memories of many fans today but "Ozark Ike", as he was called because of his resemblance to the comic strip character, sent 29 balls out of the park in 1950. From 1951 to 1957, the White Sox outfielder would be second only to Mickey Mantle in homeruns in the American League. The opposite of Zernial, both in appearance and style of play, was the Philadelphia Athletics left-handed first baseman, Ferris Fain. Fain was a hard-nosed player who hated to lose and who could develop a severe case of the 'red ass' with minimal encouragement. With a mitt on his right hand, he could play sacrifice bunts very aggressively and throw out runners at second base. At the end of his career, he would rank third all-time in assists for a first baseman. A choke-hitter in contrast to Zernial's end of the knob grip on the bat, Fain with less power usually had an on-base percentage of .40 or higher (on-base at least four of every ten at bats). He would later win American League batting titles in 1951 and 1952.

Among the new crop of All-Stars, Bob Lemon was especially noteworthy. He originally was a position player, but in 1948, he entered Cleveland's pitching rotation. On June 30 that year, he threw a no-hitter against the Tigers. That year was to be his first of seven straight seasons as an All-Star player. Despite his pitching prowess though, Lemon was convinced that he was a hitter. Lou Boudreau, the manager of the Indians, usually let Lemon hit for himself because his bat was too important to lose. Eventually he would rank second all-time in number of homeruns by a pitcher. Lemon frequently was among league leaders in complete games, innings pitched, and shut outs. But each time I shined his baseball shoes in the late 40s I noticed that the pitcher's toe plate was missing, a subtle indication of his refusal to fully assume a pitcher's identity. Right-handed

The most difficult pitcher for Joe DiMaggio to hit.

LEROY "SATCHEL" PAIGE

He won two batting titles back-to-back.

FERRIS FAIN

pitchers wore toe plates on their right shoe and southpaws wore toe plates on their left shoe to protect the inner portion of the shoe from excessive and rapid wear caused by rubbing against the pitching rubber.

I knew very little about Lemon before becoming a batboy for visiting teams at Briggs Stadium. Other players, such as Taft ("Taffy) Wright, Joe Gordon, and Frankie "the Crow" Crossetti were very familiar figures in the weekly editions of the *Sporting News* and baseball magazines. I anxiously waited during my first year as batboy for each team's first visit. Now I would see players whose stats I had been memorizing and whose exploits I had been hearing about on the radio. Crossetti, whose 37 years with the club was the longest continuous service by someone in Yankee uniform, was finishing a 17-year career as a player in 1948. He was always a reliable shortstop, usually near or at the top in most defensive categories. A modest batting average disguised the common ability of Yankee players to deliver in the clutch. He was not an easy out when the game was on the line.

"Taffy" Wright was known for his bat and would soon end his career with an overall batting average of .311. His last year as a player was with the Philadelphia Athletics in 1949, after spending most of his time with the White Sox, with years out for military service. Never a gazelle in the outfield, he more than paid for his roster spot with crisp line drives to all fields. Wright deserves mention because he won the American League batting title in his rookie season, 1938, by compiling a robust .350 average. Thereafter, in 1941 he collected an RBI in 13 consecutive games. Sadly, for Wright, his batting title was erased in 1951 when number of at bats, instead of game appearances, was accepted as the new standard with no grandfather clause to recognize his accomplishment under previous rules.

Nineteen forty-eight was a banner year for the Cleveland Indians as they were led by a handful of players who never would equal their performances that season. Most challenges were met and overachievement typically was the order of the day for many players. Joe Gordon, a smooth fielding, long ball-hitting second baseman exemplified the sustained high level of play by Cleveland battling for championship honors. Gordon already was an established All Star when he arrived from the Yankees in a trade for Allie Reynolds, who in turn, became the anchor of the New York pitching staff in 1947. In fact, Gordon had been chosen the American League's MVP in 1942 instead of triple crown (batting average, home runs, runs-batted in) winner, Ted Williams. In the championship run of 1948, Gordon set the American League's season home run record for second base-men with 32 four-baggers. His 246 career home runs also would be a record for his day, and yet his preference was for fielding rather than for hitting. Saying one day in the pre-game clubhouse: "You hit the ball and it goes somewhere and then you're through, but fielding, that's something else. Fielding is a blend of rhythm, finesse, teamwork and balance." These remarks would deeply affect, from then

Thought of himself as a hitter, not a pitcher, and wouldn't wear a toe plate.

BOB LEMON

on, how I watched and appreciated baseball. A 15-year old boy only wants to hit the long ball. Gordon could do that with relative ease while recognizing that good defensive play was at the heart of what appeared to be a simple game.

Few people who saw him perform would deny that Joe DiMaggio epitomized grace and fluid movement as he flawlessly executed difficult defensive plays. DiMaggio's skill as a centerfielder could be appreciated best when watching his contemporaries. They strained to make breath-taking catches against the wall in the power alleys in right-center and left-center fields. The Yankee Clipper instinctively broke at the crack of the bat toward the spot where the ball would arrive. He always seemed to know exactly how much speed was needed to make the play effortlessly.

DiMaggio entered the clubhouse before games early enough to sit and read the newspaper while enjoying a smoke or two. Teammates treated him with the courtesy and respect reserved for a player of his stature. They gave him as much privacy as possible in a crowded clubhouse environment. During pre-game practice, he took occasional cigarette breaks, and even later, between innings, he was joined by others, and the occasional umpire, in the dugout tunnel for a quick puff. So much for the myth that smoking reduced athletic ability!

DiMaggio usually was last to leave the clubhouse after games, as he waited for crowds of adoring fans to head for the exits. He sat in front of his locker before and after his shower, as he followed the post game ritual of quiet introspection, drinking beer, and lighting one cigarette with still one more. While clubhouse boys and batboys began to hang sweaty undergarments in the dryer, mop the floors, swab the toilets, and shine game shoes for another day, DiMaggio dressed in this gray double-breasted suit, conservative tie, and highly polished black shoes. He walked slowly out of the clubhouse, bidding Fat Frank good evening, hailed a cab, and usually left alone.

Cornelius McGillicuddy, A.K.A. Connie Mack, also was an iconic figure of the national pastime in the late forties and early fifties. His contributions as a player, manager, and owner of some of the American League's best and worst teams during the 20th century made him an inseparable part of baseball's image in American society. By the late forties, son Earle carried the daily responsibilities of manager and link with the players. Earle sat next to his octogenarian father on the bench during games and went to the mound to remove the pitchers who needed replacement.

Mr. Mack, as he was politely addressed by players and others, would arrive at the clubhouse by himself, tall and straight in posture, and wearing a dark blue suit with detachable, highly-starched shirt collar and dark hat and shoes. After a few quick words with Earle, he went to the dugout without changing into uniform to watch pre-game practice. Once the game began Mr. Mack conversed quietly

No one had more pride in his performance than the Yankee Clipper.

JOE DIMAGGIO

with Earle and positioned defensive players, by waving his scorecard, according to situation and the pitch count. The foul-mouthed banter common to dugouts during a game was absent in his presence. Any player using profanity, even in exasperation, was cautioned by other players to watch their language in front of the tall tactitian, as he had been referred to by the media years before (the Ol' Man as he was referred to by the players). Most of the team respected Mack and played hard for him, for example Pete Suder, journeyman 2nd baseman and one of Mack's personal favorites for most of a decade.

One day, after flying out in his last at bat and going one for four, Suder hustled back to the bench expressing his frustration with obscenities:

"Goddammit, can't I ever get more than one hit in a game?"

Followed by Mack's soothing replay:

"Now, now, Peter. Patience. You're too good a player to let emotion keep you from helping the team."

After the game, Cornelius McGillicuddy was a solitary figure as he made his way slowly through the tunnel, across the clubhouse, and out of the ballpark.

The tall tactician in his game uniform

CONNIE MACK

Chapter 5

Rubbers and Chocolates

"Baseball is the only field of endeavor where a man can succeed
three times out of ten and be considered a good performer."
Often overheard in the clubhouse and in the dugout, and wherever
people would listen—Ted Williams's view of success as a hitter.

"Hoot" Robinson's taxi stand, maintenance garage, and short-order restaurant
stood on Trumbull Ave. across the street from the right field grandstand of Briggs
Stadium. Home runs that left the park over the third deck followed a trajectory
leading to the roof of "Hoot's" establishment. By 1999, 22 sluggers had accomplished the feat and Ted Williams was the first to do it. Services for taxi fleets
occupied most of the multistoried building, except for the elongated public eating
section with counter and stools on the Michigan Ave. side. Although it lacked
a gourmet menu and seafood entrees, "Hoot's" place served wholesome food in
quantity for a reasonable price. Ball players with big appetites before and after
games frequently ordered from a variety of mouthwatering sandwiches and slices
of pie. Fans attending Tiger games could step off the streetcar and into Robinson's
for a quick bite.

"Hoot's" place had a high energy level 24 hours a day. Customers from all
segments of society rubbed shoulders and talked baseball on the counter stools,
or while holding their plates and leaning against the wall when no seats were
available. If batboys arrived to pick up or to place orders for the players, "Hoot"
made sure that they received prompt attention. The man knew how to fill stom-
achs and move satisfied customers in and out. Fat Frank consumed as much of
"Hoot's" food over the years as anyone and his appearance offered ample evidence
of his desperate affection for roast beef sandwiches on white bread—with a slice

or two of pie. For some ball players, Robinson's café represented an oasis of eating pleasure.

Perhaps one of the funniest situations I witnessed from the dugout involved a display of consummate gluttony by one of the most entertaining players in the American League at the time—Paul "Dizzy" Trout. He was listed in the Tiger guidebook at 6'2" and 195 lbs., a weight long since increased, as advancing years and decreased attention to proper nutrition took their toll. Trout's stomach expanded outward and gravity caused his gut to droop over his belt. He, nevertheless, was an effective and hard-working component of the Tiger pitching staff for 13 years while hitting with power (20 career homeruns). Trout not only was a source of humor, but wore glasses when he pitched (before shatter-proof lenses). A red handkerchief always stuck out of his pants pocket when he was on the mound. As part of his preparation in the clubhouse on days he was the starting pitcher, Trout would wolf down two of "Hoot's" sizable pork chop sandwiches chased by a bottle or two of carbonated beverage. Then he went out to the bullpen for pregame warm-up tosses.

My day's work had already begun, and I was waiting to retrieve the third batter's lumber. On this day, Trout's fastball was effective in wiping out the first two batters. I crouched down on the second step of the visitor's dugout near the bat rack permitting the manager an unobstructed view of home plate. Trout bent over to get the catcher's sign for the next pitch. He hesitated … peered intently toward the plate … shook off the catcher's sign for one he liked better. He leaned over even more. His left hand was on his left thigh, the ball behind his back in his right hand, and then it happened—a prodigious belch erupted from his mouth spewing tobacco juice across the front of the white home jersey with the Old English D. Only fans in seats behind the plate witnessed the hilarious occurrence and noticed the startled Tiger catcher, Bob Swift, rock back on his heels. The batter jumped back and out of the batter's box.

The umpire removed his mask. "Time!" he shouted through his laughter.

Swift yelled, "Jesus Christ, Dizz!" Did you puke on yourself?"

"No, but Hoot's pork chops sure taste better the second time around."

By this time, all the visiting players in the dugout behind me were laughing uncontrollably at 'Dizzy's' antics on the mound. But 'Dizz' and the pork chops prevailed as the Tigers won with the help of Al Benton in short relief.

This was, by no means, the only instance of crude baseball humor. Pranks eased boredom and were part of welcoming rituals for rookies joining the ball club. During the stifling heat of August, bench-riding players on teams long out of the pennant race would apply the "hot foot" to a sleeping comrade or inattentive rookie. A kitchen match would be inserted gently into the sole of the sleeper's spikes and then lit to burn quickly and rouse him into consciousness with unexpected

Often good for a laugh and part of the Tigers' fearsome TNT
(Trucks, Newhouser, Trout) pitching rotation.

DIZZY TROUT

pain. An especially effective means of sending a welcoming message to young new comers or to silence chronic bitchers was the "hot" jockstrap. Liberal amounts of Bengay were rubbed into at least one, if not all, of the target's jockstraps before pregame practice. Not until pores opened with the onset of perspiration did the medicinal aid make its presence known. With confined testicles aflame, the player would dash frantically into the clubhouse and take a quick half shower for lower extremities. When the fire had been extinguished another seemingly fresh jock-strap was put on for the game. But it also had been treated and soon testicles were burning again. Other players usually acted as though nothing was wrong. The game seemed to lend itself easily to bouts of levity, despite the tension of close pennant races and certain ritual behavior by the players. No matter how friendly the confines of the ball yard, fans usually were unaware of what was actually being said on the field or between players on the field and those in the dugouts.

From the beginning of a game one day with the Red Sox, bench jockeys were fine-tuning their insults and innuendos in response to nonstop chatter and whining by Tiger first baseman, George "The Greek" Vico. Vico had modest skills and occasionally hit with power, but enjoyed doing the splits with great flourish when thrown balls arrived at first on close plays. Opposing players normally took pleasure in "gently" teasing him about his antics, but this day, the exaggerated gymnastics triggered a heated response from the bench. Vico continued a rapid-fire barrage of insults peppered with his best social barbs in Greek, while the batter ran the count to three balls and two strikes. Then from just behind me, Johnny Pesky issued the final ultimatum. "Shut the fuck up you big Greek bastard. If you don't, we'll have Danny, our batboy, kick your ass up between your shoulder blades, and if he can't do it, then the Jap kid will." He was pointing at Masi Sakow, the Japanese clubhouse boy who was perched on the top step at the other end of the dugout. Upon hearing himself placed in challenge, Masi jumped into the tunnel and hid near the grungy urinal, much to the delight of the players in the dugout.

Major league ball clubs in the late 40s and early 50s imposed dress codes for ball players on road trips. They were expected to appear in public wearing suits or jackets—usually with ties and dress shirts. A few sported straw hats in season, some chose a felt fedora. There were, of course, a handful of nonconformists with an aversion to cravats or any kind of attire suggesting the proper businessman. Ted Williams's celebrity gave him membership in the latter group. His conces-sion to formal dress was a suit, but with a short-sleeved sport shirt opened at the neck and it's collar worn outside the lapels of his suit coat, and certainly not a hat. "Those are for candy asses," he boomed, when chided good naturedly by players he respected.

Whenever the Red Sox visited Detroit, Ted Williams always was the first ball player to arrive at the clubhouse. He came through the sliding door at a gallop and headed straight to his locker with a nod of the head to Fat Frank and a quick, "How the hell are ya, Frank? Gettin' laid?"

Williams didn't need to ask where his locker was. He took it for granted that the best visitor's clubhouse in the American League would remember to put his gear in the same spot as always—far down along the left wall of lockers next to the catchers, where he and "Birdie" Tebbetts could chatter back and forth, and also across from the trainer's room.

"Johnny, where the hell are my goddamned bats?" Johnny was Johnny Orlando, Boston's clubhouse man and Williams's traveling sycophant. It was his responsibility to look after and to protect the most treasured of Williams's possessions during the baseball season. Not his gloves. Not his spikes. Not his favorite sweatshirts or his jockstraps. But his bats. His bats were a direct extension of the man himself. If runners of track and cross-country defined themselves as running objects, then Ted Williams identified himself as a scientific hitter of spheroid horsehides.

Hitting baseballs was the most important thing in life for Williams, when he wasn't fishing. He arrived at the "office" bubbling over with enthusiasm for the day's contest and eager to begin his mental and physical preparations. Without waste of time or movement, Williams would change from street clothes to pre-game clubhouse garb as quickly as a comic book super hero would change identity. Sweatshirt, jock strap, and shower clogs quickly became costume for the daily ritual leading to batting practice when the Red Sox replaced Tiger players on the field. Orlando would place an armful of bats in the locker for Williams to inspect, both visually and by hefting each one separately. Dirt and resin, which had accumulated from the previous game, were removed carefully by rubbing each bat on a soup bone. Williams insisted on boning his working tools to prevent impurities from adding unwanted weight to his usual 34-ounce bats. He customarily kept six or seven bats ready at all times, some as light as 32 ounces.

Williams possessed an uncanny ability to heft a bat and judge it's weight. He once shouted at Orlando, "Johnny, why the hell did you order 35s (ounces) from the company? They know my specs."

Orlando replied, "I didn't. You saw the order yourself."

By this time, Birdie Tebbetts chimed in with support for Orlando. "Let me feel the damned thing. It's a 34 and you're full of shit," he proclaimed as he took a turn hefting the bat. "Get off Johnny's back."

But Williams was insistent and bellowed, "Bring me a fuckin' scale and I'll prove it's a 35."

Baseball's greatest hitter—he said so.

TED WILLIAMS

Tebbetts wouldn't give up either. "Use the scale to weigh your bullshit, Williams."

Williams soon put the bat on the scale and the dial showed—you guessed it—35 ounces! "See, Tebbetts. You wouldn't know shit if I didn't tell you," Williams gloated. "We just keep you on the ballclub to help your pension."

Such exchanges were not unique and kept the clubhouse loose as most players marveled at Williams's expertise, which he was ever ready to display.

How I enjoyed the tremendous opportunity to be a fly on the wall and listen to Williams's lectures during each visit to Detroit. Whenever possible, I sat on a trunk in the middle of the clubhouse or kept my ears open while mopping floors or swabbing toilets as he expanded his usual catechism of hitting to include fundamentals of stance and swing, body movement, and gripping the bat. Williams always contended that a slight upswing, led by hips rotating around and upward, kept the bat longer in the impact zone. Some players at the time disagreed and favored a level or a downward swing. Williams repeatedly insisted that hip-cocking was as important as wrist action during the bat's swing, if not more so. "If you want to hit with power, get your goddamned butt into the ball," was his advice. In other words, a batter generated power from rotation of hips into the ball. The wrist, at impact with the ball, was square as though swinging an ax into a tree as the batter pushed the right (or left) hand through the impact area to make contact with the ball. Therefore, the top wrist broke only a little and didn't roll over or break during the swing, according to Williams. The top hand would be in the strongest possible position with the wrist unbroken and behind the ball at the time of impact.

However, the longer a batter could wait for the ball, the less chance he would be fooled by a pitch and the better his chances of introducing one "joy spot" to another, using an upward arc of swing to intersect the downward arc of the pitched ball. The "fat" part of the bat or "joy spot" was a 4-1/2 inch section near the end and would meet the 3/4 inch "joy spot" on the ball at 90 degrees from the direction of the pitch. When he wasn't expounding on the science of hitting, Williams sat on his stool, on a trunk, or strolled around the clubhouse squeezing rubber balls or hand grips in each hand and doing finger push-ups on the floor, where space permitted, to strengthen his arms, hands, shoulders, legs, and back. Although the arc of swing was important, body strength completed Williams' equation for successful hitting.

"In the batter's box," Williams cautioned, "never swing until you see the pitcher's fast ball which allows you to better judge the speed of other pitches. Be sure you make that son of a bitch on the mound throw the ball as much as possible. The higher the pitch count for every batter, the sooner the pitcher may get tired. Also, the first at-bat is the game's most important because the batter gets the must useful information about the pitcher."

Williams would conclude by saying that his strike zone was 7 balls wide and 11 balls high including the balls at the corners of the imaginary vertical plane over the plate. He insisted that batters know their "happy zones"—where their swing was most productive. His "happy zone" began half way up the strike zone and reached to the top of it, making him a better hitter against high "heat," "alto queso," or the "high hard one." Whereas some hitting coaches wanted batters to keep their arms away from the body, Williams disagreed and recommended a distance of 3 to 8 inches. He held the bat upright and almost vertical to the ground because he maintained the bat felt lighter and more comfortable in this position. Besides, he said, "holding the bat in the vertical position puts more of a loop into the arc of swing."

No one could say Ted Williams lacked self-confidence. He became the most potent hitter of his era by realizing that the essential requirements for continued high level of achievement were tireless effort and constant study of hitting added to his immense natural talents. Twenty-ten vision and unmatched eye/hand coordination allowed him to excel at hitting a baseball—in his words, "the single most difficult thing to do in sport."

When he was satisfied with the condition of his bats for the game, he began a daily ritual to prepare mentally for the day's contest and to examine his swing for any hitches or undesirable tendencies. He stood in front of the clubhouse mirror, clad only in sweatshirt, jock strap, and shower clogs to get the best view of his batting stance and swing.

"My name is Ted Fucking Williams and I'm the greatest hitter in baseball."—SWING. "My name is Ted Fucking Williams and I'm the greatest hitter in baseball."—SWING. He repeated this mantra relentlessly. The routine was interrupted only by occasional orations on the finer points of hitting for anyone who cared to listen. Included in the Williams lecture were repeated references to his "rules of hitting:

1. Only swing at strikes.
2. Never swing at a pitch that you have trouble hitting or that fools you.
3. With two strikes on you, forget about hitting the long ball. Shorten up on the bat, try to put the head of the bat on the ball.
4. And, goddamn it, don't swing at ball four! Take a walk."

(Williams would note after he retired that his proudest achievement was the large number of bases on balls he received.) Some teammates took advantage of the free lessons and joined in a dialogue with the obsessed slugger, some read the newspaper, others groused about not being in the day's starting lineup or trudged into the trainer's room for a pregame taping and a rub down. Here and there, a bored .230 hitter sat picking his nose, while starring vacantly toward the ceiling.

One day during the 1949 season, upon completing his preparation ritual, Williams returned to his locker, thought for a moment and hollered in my direction, "Hey, kid! I want you to do something for me."

I was hurrying to put finishing touches on the remaining spikes I was supposed to shine for the day. Smudges of black shoe polish on my Detroit sweatshirt and caked polish under my fingernails showed the intensity of last minute chores before batting practice.

"Yessir, Mr. Williams," I said. Batboys never called players by their first names, even if requested to do so. This was a rule of behavior not to be broken in the American League's best visitor's clubhouse. "What do you want?" I continued, thinking that he might be hungry for a hot dog from the concession stand across from the clubhouse. Ah, but no. He was about to send me on the most memorable errand in my experience as a batboy.

"Here's $35," he explained. "Take a cab downtown and get me the best five-pound box of chocolates you can find and a <u>big</u> box of rubbers. Can you do that for me, kid? This is very important. I've got a heavy date this weekend. Don't let me down."

"No sir," I said. "You'll have them before game time." I heard myself saying the words, but I was thinking, "Oh Jesus, the drug store will never sell rubbers to a 15-year old kid."

When Fat Frank found out the nature of Williams's request, he grinned and asked, "Can ya handle it?" My apparent confidence didn't fool him, and he added words of encouragement as I left the clubhouse through the sliding door. "You'll never get the rubbers, kid, and Williams'll be pissed. He'll kick your ass into next week. Ha!"

In the quick ride downtown to Woodward Ave. in a Checker Cab, my stomach turned over, and everything I had eaten that day flew back into my throat. I was more nervous than the first day I had arrived at the Visitor's Clubhouse door the year before. Failure was not an option. The cab dropped me off at Fanny Farmer's candy store on Woodward Ave. in the heart of Detroit's finest shopping district. I rushed in, still wearing telltale evidence of the morning's cleanup chores on my clothes. My mission made me oblivious to the well-dressed shoppers around me as I carefully checked the shelves for the best five-pound box of chocolates. There it was, in all its glory, in the store window, wrapped with a large red ribbon tied in a bow. Half of my errand was now complete.

That was the easy part of the journey. Now I had to convince the pharmacist in the Rexall Drugstore on the corner to release a large box of rubbers from safe keeping behind the counter. My face was on fire with embarrassment as I walked to the rear of the store toward the pharmacist behind the counter, carrying the best five-pound box of chocolates. All eyes turned to follow the grubby-looking kid down the aisle. The pharmacist asked if I wanted a prescription filled. I shook my head and asked for a small piece of paper to tell him what I wanted. I explained that I was running an errand of great importance for a ball player at Briggs Stadium and that I needed a big box of rubbers.

Such a request from a 15-year old caused the pharmacist to chuckle and ask, "You're kidding, aren't you?"

Now, even more embarrassed, I suddenly blurted out, "Call my boss and check it out, please. I will be in trouble if I go back with only half of my errand completed."

"Okay, kid. I guess there's a first time for everything," and he reached for the telephone. He contacted Fat Frank at the clubhouse and smiled as they talked briefly. He turned back to me and said, "Alright, kid. You get your big box of rubbers. This must be a very heavy date. Who's the woman?" Then I remembered the warning sign in the Visitor's Clubhouse—"What you hear here, leave here"—and pleaded ignorance.

Elated by such a favorable outcome of the errand, Danny, the best five-pound box of chocolates with red ribbon tied in a bow, and the large sack filled with a big box of rubbers headed back to Briggs Stadium in a Checker Cab. When I arrived at the clubhouse, Fat Frank greeted me. "Well kid, you got your rubbers, didn't you? That was pretty slick to convince the pharmacist to call me. Put everything on the top shelf in Ted's locker." (Fat Frank was permitted to use first names.)

When Williams returned from batting practice and looked into his locker, he yelled across the room, "Hey kid! What the hell is this?" He was holding up an envelope which had been resting next to the chocolates and the rubbers.

"I put your change there from the $35 you gave me," I explained, walking over to his locker.

Williams looked surprised. "Well I'll be goddamned. This is the only fuckin' time I ever got money back from an errand. People usually keep what's left as a tip."

The rapid trip downtown and the stratagem to score the rubbers did wonders for my self esteem and I responded quietly, "Mr. Williams, we want this to be the best visitor's clubhouse in the American League."

"Well," he replied, "it sure as shit is, kid. Here. You keep the money for yourself." ($6.50—more than twice a day's pay.)

Chapter 6

How Could I Be Washed Up So Young?

"The hardest thing is not making the big league,
Rather it is staying there"—Walter Alston in the
Complete Baseball Guide (Walter Alston)

I didn't realize when I took off my Tiger uniform after the last home game in September 1950 that someone else would be wearing it and using my locker the following year. When I was told in March 1951 not to report to the visitor's clubhouse for the season soon to begin, I was crushed. I felt rejected by everyone. Then I knew how ball players must have felt after being traded when they had played many years for one team. A sinking sensation in my stomach switched on a wave of anxiety, and I tried not to accept my fate that it was over. There was no appeal.

I knew immediately that no amount of pleading would get my job back. Fat Frank obviously was not supportive, and his boss was big Al Julian in charge of stadium operations. Big Al had the warmth of a meat locker and certainly wouldn't champion my cause. His response to any pleas for reconsideration of my sacking likely would be an abrupt, "Tough shit, kid! You had three years. Go home!" A letter from Mother, which she would insist on writing, or a phone call from Dad would not give me traction with big Al, and Fat Frank would simply munch on another candy bar and smile. Mother never really wanted to grasp the realities of ballpark society. Dad saw it as something different from his everyday world. In the 1950s people accepted the reality of their situation and I wasn't a whiner. Reluctantly I was beginning to realize that a career as a major league ballplayer was nothing but a teenager's fantasy. I couldn't hit a good bender, or curveball, and I ran too long in the same place. Sandlot games probably were all I could look forward to for recreation. Acceptance of my fate was neither easy nor immediate.

Ironically my descent from the big leagues was completed in a pick-up game on a public diamond in Palmer Park adjacent to Woodward Avenue and Six Mile Road. Some asshole from the East Side—East Eight Mile Road, no doubt—stole my glove when I was standing on second base, after hitting a frozen rope into left center field to drive in two runs. Why not ask for an autograph instead? I could have supplied Inky Feller, Lou Boudreau, or others of choice. Alas fame was fleeting—in a little more than six weeks. I wondered how I would be received back into the world of mere mortals now that my life as batboy and its celebrity had ended. The finality of losing the world's greatest job—from a teenager's view-point—fueled constant anxiety.

I dreaded going to school and telling everyone why I was in afternoon classes for the first time in anyone's memory. Did failure at Briggs Stadium mean that none of the prettiest girls would want to walk with me between classes? Who wants to be seen eating lunch with a non-celebrity? There would be no difficulty reentering neighborhood society as a former major leaguer because there were few teenagers, or adults, who had been impressed by my change in life style three years earlier. Once my dear friends at the Astor Court apartments moved away, only friendships at Northwestern High School, miles distant by bus, broke the isolation of inner city life in a quickly changing neighborhood along West Grand Boulevard, three doors from Hitsville, U.S.A.(Motown Records).

Some players might finish their careers in the minor leagues, maybe in the Triple A league, hoping to be recalled to the "bigs." But this opportunity wasn't available for washed up batboys. Imagine! Seventeen years old and a has-been. If there was a good side to all of this, it was the reason that I would no longer be on the field at Briggs Stadium. I had lost my job because I looked too much like a ball player—my uniform belonged to Harvey Riebe, the Tigers' bullpen catcher. Why did I drink so much milk, eat so much bacon, and lift weights so regularly. I became bigger, stronger, and wasn't invited back.

Years later, people would ask me what were my favorite visiting teams and players and why so and which team uniforms did I like best. It may seem odd, but I always liked the St. Louis Browns and their brown-grey uniforms. Probably because I followed the Cardinals as well during the World War II period, when both teams were successful and my roots were in southern Illinois, where fan allegiance is directed toward St. Louis and not Chicago. The light bluish-grey uni-forms, blue caps and blue stirrup hose of the Philadelphia Athletics would have to rank second, with the other five American League visiting clubs grouped far behind. Road uniforms of the Yankees, Red Sox, Indians, White Sox and Senators competed with each other to have the drabbest appearance. None of the League's other seven ball clubs, however, had a home uniform equal to the Tigers's rich black and white with its old English D.

Although I didn't have direct contact with Tiger players, nevertheless I had personal favorites for their performance on the field. You see I could not root openly for the Tigers when I was on the visitor's side of the field. And besides, if the Tigers lost a series of two of three games or three of four games, or even better, if a team swept the Tigers in a series, I received bigger tips from happy winners. The tips were especially pleasant when compared to the three dollars a day given to batboys. You couldn't have much of a social life with wages that low! The best tippers at the end of the season were the best players who recognized that the boys worked hard to make the visitor's clubhouse at Briggs Stadium better than the others in the American League. Lou Boudreau, Ted Williams, Joe DiMaggio, Bob Feller, for example, always were good for a "fiver" after a series and usually ten bucks on the team's last trip to Detroit for the year. Other players gave less and most players stiffed us. But we didn't work for tips. That wasn't why we were at the ballpark.

Working in the visitor's clubhouse allowed me to interact with the best players in the American League, one of whom was Ferris Fain. He was an in-your-face type of player with the Philadelphia Athletics. He hated to make an out and could not accept losing. Whenever a teammate made an amusing comment about a situation during a game, Fain often could be heard to respond to no one in particular:

"Baseball is a serious business, and I can't joke about it!" In a fit of uncontrolled anger he once kicked first base, broke his foot, and was out of action for more than a month. More than anything else, I remember him crouching at the plate, chaw in jaw, choked up on the bat, daring the pitcher to get him out. Fain, was among the last of a dying breed of player who didn't grip the bat down at the end of the handle but instead choked up in order to have better bat control.

Jerry Coleman would remain a Yankee long enough to play on six pennant winners. Only much later did I discover that he was a hero in not one but two wars. In World War II he flew almost sixty bombing missions in the southwest Pacific. He returned to the Navy during the Korean conflict flying 120 missions and was twice awarded the Distinguished Flying Cross for heroism. I learned about his wartime exploits long after listening to his malapropisms as a baseball announcer.

Coleman was installed at second base in 1949 by Casey Stengel after beating out Snuffy Stirnweiss for the position. Stengel had been Minor League Manager of the year with the Oakland Oaks the previous season when his friend George Weiss moved into the Yankee front office. Weiss put Stengel at the helm of the team that had trailed Cleveland and Boston in 1948. Thus began the greatest string of pennant runs in baseball history, and I was there to see the beginning as Stengel led the Yankees to the first of five straight pennants. From reading the Sporting News and every baseball book I could find, I knew Stengel was a former player with modest skills who as player and as manager was a jokester and not taken seriously. When he first walked into the clubhouse at Briggs Stadium in summer 1949, I thought that he wouldn't look at all good in New York home pinstripes. Visiting grey seemed more appropriate, but you couldn't ignore his bowed legs that seemed ill-suited to forward movement.

Nevertheless, 1949 probably was his best display of managerial skills because DiMaggio didn't play until the end of June as his heel injury kept him out of the lineup. Just as the year before, the 1949 season went down to the line with the Yankees edging the Red Sox by one game and reclaiming the pennant won by Cleveland in 1948. Stengel said of his accomplishment in words typically his that

"I could'na dun it without my players."

Ten pennants and seven World Series victories in twelve years certainly were not the work of a buffoon, but of a manager who was a very good judge of talent. Many people forget that Stengel ignored much criticism to let Larry Berra learn the rudiments of catching in the majors rather than in the minors. His biographer, Roger Creamer, felt that Stengel possessed intuitive understanding of a situation and could make decisions rapidly without being deterred by analysis. An illustration would be his ability to platoon players at just the right time and to get the most from them in a given game situation.

Despite his successes Stengel wasn't a favorite of Yankee players and some were happy to see him leave after losing the 1960 World Series to the Pirates. Players had been grumbling since the late forties and early fifties about his incessant tinkering with lineups. Often during his inaugural season, proud and pompous Yankees made caustic remarks about the bowlegged clown who had replaced likeable Bucky Harris. Posting the lineup for the day on the dugout wall was sure to cause mutterings of disgust and frustration. The grumblings may have worsened throughout the fifties even with unmatched success, because Stengel's sarcasm and barbed critical comments hurt feelings not repaired. The visitor's clubhouse crew at Briggs Stadium always gave extra effort for the Bronx Bombers, yet Stengel barely acknowledged that we were busting our butts for the Yankees—the best working for the best.

Ned Garver was the Greg Maddux of his era who always toiled for bad teams in a shorter career. Garver was one of only seven pitchers in history to win twenty

No manager beat the Ol' Perfesser in a game of smarts.

CASEY STENGEL

games for a last place club. He also was the sole player to win twenty games and hit over .300 for a team losing a hundred or more games. Seldom was Garver removed for a pinch-hitter, and he often batted sixth.

His contributions didn't go unnotice. He finished second to Yogi Berra in the voting for the American League's Most Valuable Player award in 1951, a year when his victories accounted for over thirty-eight percent of the Brown's wins, when he pitched an astounding total of twenty-four complete games! I'm surprised that St. Louis didn't erect a monument recognizing achievements that passed largely without acclaim. Yet to those who were privileged to watch him perform, as I was, Ned Garver was the total package.

Ellis Kinder, or "Old Folks" as he was known, arrived late in the big leagues and still managed to leave his mark. A thirty-year old rookie, he later led the American League in won-lost percentage and shutout games, feats which almost led the Red Sox to the pennant in 1949. At first a stalwart member of the Boston's starting rotation Kinder then became a skilled reliever who set a record of twenty-seven saves. Old Folks was totally confident with a quiet manner, from his arrival in the clubhouse in business suit and tie, until he took the mound to challenge the rivals of the day.

Like all teenage boys at the time I had my own special list of superheroes in baseball. Some individuals, however, fell from the list once I watched them perform for three seasons, and others took their places. Inclusion in my list was based completely upon performance and achievements supported by comparison of statistics. That is, until I saw Lou Brissie the tall left-hander of the Philadelphia Athletics. Today he could qualify for a handicapped person's parking space in the player's area of the parking lot. But in the late forties and early fifties, Brissie received no special consideration.

Nevertheless, he was a marvel of survival as he played not only with a brace on one leg, but also an artificial leg in addition. Loss of one leg and crippling injury to the other were injuries received when he was fighting in Italy during World War II. Although his career was relatively short, it was testament to his determination to play in the major leagues, regardless of personal cost. His best years were 1949-50, when he was an important part of Connie Mack's starting staff. Brissie went to the top of my list of heroes on just physical courage alone. He had greater agility on the mound than some pitchers with two good legs.

The Athletics at this time enjoyed a brief period of success as Connie Mack was able to put together a small competitive band of journeyman ballplayers who had several productive seasons for him. Among this group was bespectacled Eddie Joost who joined the A's after a less than mediocre ten-year career and a return to the minor leagues. He returned to the bigs with newly discovered power at the plate and an uncanny ability to draw bases on balls as a leadoff man. He would

The total package for a losing team, he could do everything well on the baseball field.

NED GARVER

Better on half a leg than many two-legged players

LOU BRISSIE

average more than one hundred walks for six consecutive seasons as Philadelphia's shortstop and became a threat on offense. I had never heard of Eddie Joost until I arrived at Briggs Stadium, yet it was obvious that, in the words of some observers, he transformed the A's into a contender with his reliable, and at times, exceptional performance.

Lou Brissie wasn't the sole returnee from World War II who made important contributions to the post-war A's. "Fidgity Phil" Marchildon was a good pitcher for mostly non-competitive teams. And even though he walked more batters than he struck out, his career earned run average was under 4.00. Pitching coaches were unable to change his throwing motion, which reduced his effectiveness on the mound. Throwing across his body robbed him of greater control. When I quietly asked one of the A's coaches during a game why Marchildon used this kind of delivery, he indicated by the look on his face that he had given up recommending changes. Then we heard the plate umpire yell ball four. The coach said,

"Here we go again."

But when you remember that Marchildon survived a German prisoner of war camp and came directly back to the big leagues, criticism of his way of playing suddenly seemed less important.

Jeff Heath was one of my favorite ball players before my years at the ballpark. I had heard that his first full season as a regular for the Indians brought colossal results of 112 RBIs, a slugging percentage of .602, and a .343 batting average. These stats were enough to make a star of him on the board baseball games made for kids and especially popular in the mid-forties when my enthusiasm for baseball was beginning to surge. He then was patrolling the outfield of the St. Louis Browns with the likes of Walt Judnich and Chet Laabs. Heath remained on my short list of heroes until many decades later, when I came upon information that confirmed how unfairly the first black players were treated in the major leagues.

The same year that Larry Doby signed with Cleveland (1947), Negro League slugger, Willard Brown, whose accomplishments some said, rivaled those of the great Josh Gibson, and fellow black Hank Thompson, joined the Browns. Willard Brown literally stopped off in the white American League for a cup of coffee. He hit only .179 with one homerun in twenty-one games. The lone four-bagger though provided a link to Jeff Heath and his petulant display of prejudice toward a teammate.

Brown liked to use a very heavy bat and found one discarded by Jeff Heath that had its knob broken off. Pleased with its heft, Brown decided to tape the knob back onto the bat. The plate umpire, however, disqualified the wood when Brown went to hit with it. Tape and knob were removed and Brown promptly hit a home

His only major league homerun prompted a racial response

WILLARD BROWN

run that was the first by a black player in the American League and the only one in his career. Heath was neither pleased nor amused by the incident and broke the bat, presumably to erase any evidence of his teammate's achievement. Brown soon vanished from the major leagues while Thompson went on to play with the New York Giants.

Hulking and powerful Luke Easter was so strong that his sweat must have had muscles. A short career with Cleveland was punctuated by tape-measure homeruns.

"I just hit 'em and forget 'em."

Easter would say as if his projectiles into the outfield seats were ordinary. Unfortunately for long ball fans, bad knees cut short Easter's stay in the big show. He will always be remembered for a 550-foot blast out of Buffalo's Offermann Stadium which was used for filming the classic baseball movie, *The Natural*.

One of the outstanding shortstops of the forties, one of the best defensive shortstops of all time, a very good hitter, and eight-time All-Star, Lou Boudreau would have been memorable, even if he hadn't been a fraternity brother of mine—but years earlier. Only years later did I see his picture and that of Frank Gifford plus other notables in the Phi Sigma Kappa house in Ann Arbor. Boudreau went to Illinois and Gifford to Southern California, but it was common practice for national fraternities to display their famous members to attract newcomers into the fold. Boudreau achieved early notoriety when he became the youngest major league manager at 24 years of age in Cleveland. He proved to be an innovator in baseball strategy and was best known for the "Williams Shift." The Shift positioned six players to the right of second base and used the left-fielder to play a deep shortstop. Jimmy Dykes actually had been the first manager to try the shift in 1941 when he was with the Pale Hose. But Boudreau used the defensive alignment when his game stats showed he was almost forty percent more successful against Ted Williams when using it. Moreover, Boudreau was responsible for moving Bob Lemon from the outfield to the pitchers mound and turning knuckleballer Gene Bearden into a starter. Best of all, I witnessed portions of Boudreau's colossal performance in 1948 when Cleveland shot the table and took the crown in the World Series. He hit .355 with eighteen home runs, 106 runs batted in, and a slugging percentage of .534, topped off with two home runs in the seasonal ending American League playoff against Boston.

Another favorite player has to be the hard-nosed, crew-cut, ex-Marine, who excelled in Stengel's platoon system with left-handed and right-handed hitting outfielders. Hank Bauer, whose face was described as a clenched fist, was the extreme hustler and perfect, if not relentless, Yankee who played on nine pennant winners in ten years. He always expected to win and was quoted as claiming

An innovative manager and a fine shortstop

LOU BOUDREAU

that other teams wouldn't be allowed "to screw with our money, because we're (the Yankees) going to the bank in October." His determination to excel was well illustrated in 1948 by his catch in deep right center field which drew DiMaggio's ire—he was, according to the Yankee Clipper, "the first son-of-a-bitch who ever invaded my territory." DiMaggio wanted no one to think he couldn't cover the alleys in left field and right field.

On the Tigers side of the field, my list of favorite players was much shorter. Maybe this was the result of not being in their clubhouse. Among the Tiger players, I suppose I most admired George Kell, because he played third base so well, and I also played the position. We were both about the same size my last year with the visiting teams at Briggs Stadium. He cost Ted Williams the triple-crown by winning the batting title in 1949—342911 to 342756—and I was still trying to connect with a good curve ball. For both of us, hard work and guts replaced lack of talent when necessary. A Joe DiMaggio smash broke his jaw in 1948 yet Kell crawled to third to make a force play, almost a prelude to a subsequent event when I was practicing with the Northwestern High School team. He had such good bat control that he only struck out thirteen times the year he won the batting title. No batting champion since 1910, when whiffs first were counted for hitters, had managed so few.

Another of my favorite Tigers was Virgil "Fire" Trucks, who was one third of the potent T-N-T (Trout, Newhouser, Trucks) starting rotation. His blazing fastball gave him winning seasons in all but two years in a career that carried through the forties, including military service, and into the fifties. One of his losing seasons (5-19, 1952) would have been almost a total loss except for his two no-hitters. At that time only Johnny Vander Meer, Allie Reynolds, Sandy Koufax, and Nolan Ryan also would double up their hitless games. Trucks achieved his second no-hitter when the official scorer changed an earlier hit to an error made by Johnny Pesky.

Hal Newhouser was the Hall of Fame hurler for the Tigers, during the forties and early fifties after an unpromising beginning in the big leagues. His wins began to mount when he mastered a wicked slider for his out-pitch. He and the other two members of the T-N-T Tiger rotation pitched more innings each season as both starters and relievers than many present day starting pitchers compile in one year. And they did it without arm trouble or vacations on the disabled list, a curious difference between two eras. Either T-N-T and their counterparts were supermen or they threw when their arms were sore. Team trainers, coaches, and managers generally felt that pitching arms were muscles that with proper throwing motion (mechanics) would not be injured by the total number of innings considered excessive today.

Edged out Ted Williams to win the 1949 batting title by the slimmest of margins

GEORGE KELL

Walter "Hoot" Evers filled the last slot in my small group of favorite Tigers players I watched from the visitor's side of the field for approximately two hundred thirty games during the 1948, 1949, and 1950 seasons. Interest in B-movie cowboy star Hoot Gibson was responsible for his nickname, which gave Detroit fans an opportunity to greet each appearance at the plate with enthusiastic cries of "Hoooot, Hoooot, Hoooot." For my three years at the corner of Michigan and Trumbull, Evers arguably was one of the league's best outfielders, hitting .314, .304 and a career high of .323, when he also led the league in triples and hit for the cycle (single, double, triple, and homerun), a feat accomplished by no other Tiger for forty-three years. Sadly for Detroit fans, he was traded to Boston where he was supposed to replace Ted Williams, who entered military service in the Korean War.

In 1948 the Tigers were barely above .500 and finished fifth, 18 ½ games behind the Cleveland Indians. The two following seasons the Bengals improved by nine and then eight games, respectively, in the won-loss columns, closing 1949 and 1950 in fourth place and then in second place. The best of the three seasons was 1950, when they trailed the Yankees by only two games at the end of the pennant race. As their wins increased, fans in greater numbers showed up at the ballpark,and attendance records were set and came close to the two million mark in 1950, under their new manager Red Rolfe, former Yankee third baseman. The Tigers were inactive in the trade market compared to the rest of the league and made no trades in 1950.

Maybe their exchange of Billy Pierce and cash for White Sox catcher Aaron Robinson in 1948 burned them too badly. Most Tiger fans would later see this as a trade executed by stone brains in the Detroit front office. Robinson was out of baseball in a few years, and Pierce starred in a sixteen-year career, mostly with the White Sox and ending with the Giants. The arrival of Don (Cab) Kolloway from the White Sox and Gerry Priddy from the Browns, and the long expected departure of Dick Wakefield to the Yankees, summed up the rest of the significant trades when Danny carried bats and shagged balls at Briggs Stadium.

Being declared redundant by the Tigers early in the spring meant that I suddenly had much more free time. I could study harder and get higher grades in high school. Wrong! I already had a high "B" or an "A" in all my courses. My challenge at Northwestern was athletics, not academics. Now I could at least work out with the varsity baseball squad and be team manager. I had given up playing baseball in high school to be batboy for the visiting teams at Briggs Stadium. A very good trade with no regrets. Now I could take batting practice and fielding drills with a very good bunch of guys, who would capture the Westside championship and play for the city title of Detroit. After several weeks of workouts with the Varsity, I quickly became convinced that I could have made the ball club, if

Two no-hitters in the same year, but a losing record for the season

VIRGIL TRUCKS

not as a starter, then certainly as a reserve. In a practice game with another west side school, Northwestern coach Sam Bishop, a wonderfully gruff but considerate man, put me in at third base, where I had been working out from time to time. With runners on first and second and no outs, the stage was set for a sacrifice bunt. I charged toward the plate with the pitch expecting to throw out a slow runner at second base. Maybe we could turn a double play, if everything worked well! Why not? I had a strong, accurate arm fresh from the major leagues. The first pitch was a ball. On the second pitch I charged the plate again. Everyone expected the bunt—except the batter, who apparently was playing his own private game. He swung at the pitch sending a line drive into my charging jaw (on the right side)! The ball fell to my knees, not my feet, because I had slumped to the ground. I yelled through bloody lips;

"You dumb bastard, you missed the sign, didn't you? But you're dead!"

I picked up the ball and threw hard to first, nailing the batter by the smallest of margins, as the other coach said;

"Good play, kid. You've got balls."

A practice session later in the week provided another opportunity for me to build my confidence. I was shagging balls in center field, while Coach Bishop was running a drill with a runner on second base trying to score on hits to the out-field. A line drive headed toward me, and I broke with the crack of the bat (just like the DiMaggio brothers), grabbed the ball on one hop, and came up throwing to home plate as the base runner rounded third base. The surprised runner was out "by a mile" because he hadn't taken me seriously and thought scoring was a cinch. The play caught the eye of coach Bishop, and he bellowed at no one in particular,

"Dammit, if you don't hustle in practice, don't suit up for the game! You took Danny for granted! But he's had experience in the big leagues"

Laughter greeted his comment, yet the coach made his point about dogging it in practice. He also complimented me and asked why I hadn't tried out for the team. I laughed and explained I had been too busy working in the American League's best visitor's clubhouse. No question that playing for the west side champs would have been exciting. My destiny though had been to spend three delightful years being tutored in hitting by Ted Williams, the master, and in fielding by Joe Gordon and the DiMaggio brothers. Memories of those glory years only grew more vivid with the passing of time.

In many respects 1949 and 1950 were very eventful baseball seasons in the life of Danny the batboy. I became very ill with mumps, lost a foul ball in the glare of Briggs Stadium's new lights, chewed tobacco—not well. Just prior to the start of a long Tiger road trip well into the schedule in 1949, I fell ill. Several days of toughing it out with an increasingly sore throat ended with a visit to the family doctor who immediately sent me to bed with a severe case of mumps. They eventually affected my testicles and caused fearsome swelling. A week in bed flat on my back, legs spread wide around ice packs to reduce massive swelling below, was not the way I had wanted to use the two weeks off. I had planned to play sandlot ball while the Tigers were away. This began a pattern of illness that would follow me through later years as I became ill with flu or bad colds during vacations.

One hot, humid night I was perched on my stool adjacent to the grandstand in foul territory in right field. My responsibility was to retrieve any foul balls hit on the ground or that might strike the grandstand wall in the air then carom into right field. Basically my job was to prevent beer-loaded fans from jumping onto the field to get balls hit foul. It was necessary to stay alert and, in a sense, be another outfielder. Any pitch suddenly could be hit toward me, either by lefties, who were dead pull-hitters or by late swinging right-handed batters. Sometimes I even crouched low to the ground to be ready for players who often hit at least one ball foul in every plate appearance. This night against the Yankees, I was especially ready, when in the midst of a Tiger rally, power-hitting Vic Wertz came to the plate. I knew he would blast at least one pitch in my direction. I was even more certain after watching him put ball after ball into the short right field seats in pre-game batting practice. Suddenly he ripped a frozen rope at me, and I jumped to my feet determined to catch the screamer. And then just as quickly, I lost the ball, which was headed for a spot above my stool, in the glare of lights along the roof of the third base grandstand. I did the only sensible thing—I ducked as the ball shot into the lower grandstand behind me, much to the surprise of many fans. What an embarrassing moment; someone could have been injured, because I failed to take a chance and possibly make the catch with my face. Apparently a happy fan got a valued souvenir, and no one was carried away on a stretcher. But being a batboy meant that any day could bring new adventures.

Joe Kuhel, manager of the Washington Senators, asked me to help him with outfield practice on a wet and dreary day when playing the game was doubtful. He stood near the right field foul line with a fungo bat and exercised the outfielders with pop-ups, line drives and long high fly balls. I caught the throws back to him. This, I thought, would be a good time to attempt my first chaw of leaf tobacco and emulate my heroes, although there were only a few of them on the Senators ball club. While I caught throws for Kuhel, I carefully worked the wad around between my cheek and jaw, occasionally trying to introduce the right amount of spit for a nicotine cocktail. Everything was working well, until I was forced to jump up and to one side to snag an errant throw. Oops! Loss of concentration now made synchronized movement and chewing impossible. Instantly I began to gag, when tobacco juice entered my throat instead of leaving my mouth for the gravel under foot. A series of convulsive coughs led to a gallant display of vomiting, as I promptly rid my stomach of two ballpark franks, one soda pop, and several of mom's best chocolate chip cookies. What a disaster! The players nearby laughed and told me not to worry. Everybody puked the first time.

Eventually I would put what I learned to good use, but not until more than twenty years later. As my sons matured, they played the equivalent of Little League baseball. Coaching with my good friend, Ralph McCall, for over six seasons, including playoffs and tournaments, we led our team to a record of 44 wins and 12 losses, in no small measure, I hope, the result of teaching our sons and those of our neighbors how major leaguers played the game. Ralph and I wanted the boys entrusted to us to see that hustle and understanding the game could make playing even more fun and winning easier. We emphasized "small ball" and usually executed better than other teams. Relentless defensive practice paid off for us. We recreated game situations so that the boys wouldn't be taken by surprise by something different and could adapt easily to it. We didn't always have the best players but often had the best team as the result of preparation. As disciplined players, the boys enjoyed manufacturing runs—a walk, a bunt, a stolen base, a squeeze bunt and one run for us. Unlike many of our rivals, the boys used signals for defensive positioning and timed pickoff plays, e.g. catcher to first or second base. We constantly stressed thinking about game situations and what to do with the ball.

My oldest son Christien made himself into the most skilled bunter for his age I'd ever seen. Lacking size he decided that he could be most effective by getting a walk, stealing a base, or laying down a bunt to drive in a run. Over a three-year period he successfully executed a squeeze bunt thirteen of fourteen times. Boys with average speed learned how to get their lead off from base and pilfer the next bag—even in double steal situations. Defensively the middle infielders and third basemen learned how to react to double steal attempts. Christien resurrected the hidden ball trick long absent from professional baseball. No one beat us in a game of smarts. It was pleasing to watch the boys discover how much more fun the game could be, once they understood its complexities. Some images from this era refuse to disappear. My youngest son, Evan, had the smoothest pure swing in town and specialized in ripping line drives against the outfield fence. He might have been a star player on the varsity, if he hadn't been seduced by golf and his ability to hit a little Titlist ball into the next county. Bob Ford was the best all around player that anyone could remember and certainly of professional caliber in later years. Ralph's son, Kevin, played any position well with confidence and total hustle. And finally, Tommy Hughes hit balls onto the dirt pile for a homerun at Hopkins Park and happily shouted his patented "Ooo—waaah!!!"

Chapter 7

Michigan and Trumbull: Baseball at the Corner

"One day I was pitching against Washington and the catcher called
for a fast ball. When it got to the plate, it was so slow that two
pigeons were roosting on it. I decided to quit." From *Sporting News*
obituary of "Dizzy" Trout.

Since I first appeared with great trepidation at the door of the visitor's clubhouse, baseball has refused to remain the same. Changes have affected the appearance of the players and the ballparks, the way the game is played, the quality of play, while retaining the one dimension that makes baseball a fine art and man's closest approach to absolute truth, the ninety feet between bases. If you haven't seen the game at either the minor or major league level for at least 30 years, the first difference you might notice would be appearance of the players and the current style of wearing uniform pants adopted by many. Tastes change in sport as in society at large. Three or more decades ago uniform pants often were worn at the knee or mid-calf. Uniforms also were less form-fitting and made of heavier material. Today trendy players seem determined to pull their uniform pants down to the tops of their spikes—maybe to eventually attach a stirrup beneath the shoe. How cool would that be! The apparent sartorial goal is always to hide the team socks carrying logo colors. Do you believe freedom of choice has been carried too far?

In the late '40s and early '50s, batting helmets were not required. The hard plastic inserts, worn on the side of the cap toward the pitcher, were used by some players, but were not popular with the majority of hitters. Tobacco chewing, while still in evidence today, was the indispensable badge of a true ball player, and a real man by players of yesteryear. The purest baseball fan from many decades ago protests current use of the designated hitter in the American League and in American

League cities during inter-league play. A larger number of pitchers in the past were dependable hitters, and they at least could lay down a bunt when the situation demanded. Failure to execute the bunt and to use it as an offensive weapon in games today makes many major league teams resemble unskilled amateurs. Contrast the St. Louis Cardinals and the Chicago Cubs in recent years. The former team, despite the presence of long-ball hitters, will play "small ball" when necessary. The latter squad too often treats Chicago to repetitious ineptitude trying to bunt successfully.

Fans also should remember that there have been cyclical changes in the theory of hitting since the 1940s, and Ted Williams played in the era that followed great sluggers such as Jimmy Foxx, Lou Gehrig, and, especially, Babe Ruth. Williams's theory on hip rotation, for successful long-ball hitting, first was developed by Ruth. The Babe's rotational approach led to more strikeouts and more pitches pulled, which meant that less playing area was used by the hitter. Whereas Ruth was a Rocky Marciano-type of heavyweight hitter, Williams was the supreme technician with a bat. Patience and remarkable vision set the Splendid Splinter apart from the Babe.

Williams made better contact as a hitter than did Ruth because 20/10 vision allowed him to see the ball so well that he seldom swung at a pitch out of the strike zone. Williams always said, "Get a good ball to hit." If you wanted to hit the ball far with power then wait for a pitch in a location within the strike zone that could be hit into the air for distance. The essential ingredients for successful long-ball hitting were hip rotation, upward arc of swing, and a pitch in from the middle of the plate. But baseball would experience fundamental changes in the form of ballparks and the approach to hitting best suited to the new shapes and playing surfaces. Such ball yards were the diametric opposites of Briggs Stadium and other ballparks in my glory years of the late '40s and early '50s.

New ballparks such as Busch Memorial Stadium, Three Rivers Stadium, the Astrodome, and Royals Stadium had large cookie-cutter shapes and fast synthetic surfaces. Baseball became more a game of speed than of power. A new approach to hitting suited to the new ballparks gained popularity as the Charlie Lau theory replaced the rotational hip theory of Williams and Ruth. Fewer fly balls and strikeouts and more line drives into the outfield gaps resulted from a new way of hitting, a technique called the modern weight shift system.

The basic features of the new technique were a stance deep in the batter's box, weight concentrated on the back foot before the pitch, then a weight shift to the front foot during the stride toward the pitch. According to Lau's theory, the batter had to go back before going forward and landing on a stiff front leg. The batter's head remained down past the moment of impact. Hitters using this technique sent the ball up the middle and to the opposite field and pulled only inside pitches.

The top hand was released after impact, because the bat stayed in the hitting zone longer with Lau's approach. Release of the top hand resulted in fewer pulled balls and more of the field being used. There was no defensive shift against these hitters as with Williams in the previous era. Even this approach to hitting, however, was destined to give way to something else.

Once again, the home run swing dominates. Fewer quality pitchers on the mound, beefed-up and stronger players, smaller ball barks (replacing the circular, cookie-cutter structures), a reduced strike zone, and, some say, a livelier ball, all contributed to bring back emphasis on the long-ball. But no hitting style now seems dominant; some successful hitters are hip rotators, others prefer weight-shift, and some combine the two styles.

Except for a few standout performers, many catchers today appear unable to throw out even 30% of base runners attempting to steal. Throws sail over second base, hit the ground in front of it, or are caught by middle infielders with out-stretched arms who pull their gloves back in vain in order to tag the runner who has already reached the bag. Only a handful of catchers seem to be able to move their feet laterally instead of trying to backhand low, wide pitches. Catchers today perform their difficult task with one glove hand, and usually keep their throwing hand behind their back and out of the way, in order to protect fingers from being broken and fingernails from being torn off. Two-handed catchers previously held their right hand in position next to the glove and were prepared to make quicker throws. One-handed catching was encouraged by the introduction of a flexible hinged glove adopted by Randy Hundley in the 1960s. To be fair, catchers are not entirely to blame. Pitchers may have slow deliveries to the plate and fail to hold base runners close to the first base bag. The next game you attend or watch on TV, count the number of pitchers with good moves to first. When was the last time you saw a runner picked off at second base?

Catchers were not alone in catching the ball with one hand. Outfielders and infielders began to mimic their teammates behind the plate much to the con-sternation of those who had been taught that baseball was a two-handed game. Randy Hundley was imitated by a new breed of catchers, then slick-fielding first baseman Vic Power set the tone for other position players. Power undeniably was one of the great glove-men in baseball history as he won seven consecutive Golden Glove awards with style envied by most of his contemporaries. Not only was he brilliant and flashy with the glove, he also was a very competent hitter. Perhaps if he had not possessed both offensive and defensive skills, his legacy of the one-handed catch would have been short-lived. Power's example was reinforced by the flawless and exciting outfield play of Roberto Clemente, whose rifle arm and hitting prowess made him a perennial All-Star.

Power and Clemente both represented still another important and permanent change in baseball, namely the racial and ethnic makeup of the players. Vic Power didn't become the first black Yankee, because he was too much of a free spirit to fit the very conservative mold desired by Yankee management. His behavior failed to conform to American racial mores of the 50s when keeping company of white women by black men was unacceptable to most white people. Even though Power's off-field social life was looked at with disapproval, simple requirements of eating and sleeping were equally difficult to arrange for black players. They were segregated from their white teammates and were unable to stay at the team hotel or to eat their meals with the team, when restaurants refused to serve black patrons. Such a situation sometimes led to unusual sleeping arrangements for Power, as he usually sacked out at a local black funeral home in a comfortable plush casket. There is no question that full acceptance of, first black and then Hispanic, ball players has been the most important change in modern baseball. Cuba became the largest foreign source of ball players for the United States after Castro's overthrow of the government in 1959. Even in 1950, six pitchers went from Cuba to the Washington Senators.

Lowering the pitching mound reduced the effectiveness of pitchers. They no longer threw downhill as much to the batter. Baseball then entered an era dominated by hitters and especially the long-ball strokers. These changes also should be seen in the context of rapid expansion, when a greater number of franchises had need of many players not of major league caliber. Only 11 of the earlier members of the American and National Leagues remained after the frenzy of creating new teams. Triple A and some Double A players became major leaguers overnight, and the quality of play suffered. Decades passed as players spent less time in the minors learning rudimentary elements of the game.

Even the casual fan of today quickly notices how often outfielders ignore the cut-off man. In the late 40s and early 50s, skill in hitting the cut-off man with throws from the outfield was an expected instead of an infrequent event. Outfielders now regularly miss the cut-off man with inaccurate throws to the infield. Watching teams play today seldom provides the opportunity to see this defensive play performed well. Will it disappear entirely, if enough players arrive in the major leagues with only scant training in the basics of defensive play? In the past, outfielders at the end of an inning did not bring their gloves with them to the dugout. Until 1954, gloves were much smaller than the current "basket"-shaped glove and were left in the outfield, out of the way, until the next inning. They didn't interfere with the game; they were part of the landscape between the foul lines.

The change in baseball that surpassed all others in emotional impact, at least for Danny the Batboy, was the disappearance of baseball from Tiger Stadium. Alas,

A trend-setting, flashy fielder and dependable hitter

VIC POWER

baseball at the corner of Michigan and Trumbull Avenues ceased with the 1999 season. The once proud, respected, and highly successful franchise had reached its nadir. Tiger teams during the 1990s and into the 21st century were perennial occupants of last place and formerly glorious Tiger Stadium (Briggs Stadium, Navin Field and Bennett Field) skidded into disrepair under the ownership of the city.

Some people said that the best seat at Briggs (Tiger) Stadium was seat 1, row 1, in section 119, which would have put you just behind the low wall separating the field from the grandstand looking directly down the right field line from behind the on-deck circle. Personally, I preferred to sit higher, if I couldn't sit in the dugout. A first row seat in the upper deck gave you an unrivalled perspective of action on the field. The best seat in section 119 now is unavailable and is taken by a tree one inch in diameter and five feet tall which occupies a crack in the concrete! Other trees also have appeared here and there around the grandstand to form the beginnings of Navin's forest. Everywhere the elements of ruin aggressively announce themselves. Paint peels, girders rust, and wires droop. Brackish water stands in the tunnel leading to the American League's best visitor's clubhouse fifty years ago.

Baseball purists and die-hard Tiger fans desperately wanted renovation and restoration of the classic structure. Developers were reluctant to convert the old ball yard into a residential and entertainment center in the midst of extreme deterioration in the surrounding neighborhood. The only interested investors wanted to use the stadium for dog-racing or boxing matches, for off-road racing, or for bullfights!! Imagine the indignation of the ghosts of Ty Cobb, Charlie Gehringer and Hank Greenberg. Signs for Little Caesar's pizza and Miller beer now fade rapidly and a decrepit exterior neon sign harmonizes by weakly announcing "Tiger Stadiu." The "m" could no longer bear to be associated with failure and decay.

Yet this was the place where I learned much about life and began to mature faster in an adult world than my peers. Three years at the ballpark gave an impressionable teenager invaluable insights about interpersonal relationships with a variety of people. My experiences enabled me to see heroes as ordinary people with failings common to all. Myth and fantasy attached to baseball were removed without erasing affection for the game. Life in the clubhouse and on the ball field helping the players was like being backstage at the theater seeing how things really were. I never would be able to accept anything by appearance in the adult world again without explanation.

Working in the American League's best visitors clubhouse imprinted me with pride in doing a job well, no matter how small or insignificant. In future years my spine would tingle, when I remembered how unbelievably fortunate I was to have been taught the fundamentals of hitting by Williams and to have learned about infield play from the likes of Majeski, Pesky, and Boudreau. Very few people today can say they sat in the dugout and watched venerable octogenarian Connie Mack manage a game and move his fielders by waving his scorecard. And finally, "Hoot" Robinson's pork chop sandwiches never will be equaled. The sounds and smells of Briggs Stadium on game day forever linger in the memory of a teenage batboy as will his first streetcar ride to the Stadium and the first time he saw the sign announcing Visitor's Clubhouse—No Visitors Allowed. For Danny the Batboy, the home of the Tigers always will remain at the corner of Michigan and Trumbull Avenues.

Extra Innings

10th Inning—1948
11th Inning—1949
12th Inning—1950

Batting and pitching stats for all players on the eight teams in the American League when Danny was a batboy at Briggs Stadium, with selected highlights for each inning. Compiled by Amy Polzin.

"There is nothing greater for a human being than to get his body to react to all the things one does on the ball field. It's as good as sex; it's as good as music. It fills you up.
Buck O'Neil, Kansas City Monarch's first baseman.

1948 AMERICAN LEAGUE TEAM STANDINGS

Team	Wins	Losses	WP	GB
Cleveland Indians	97	58	.626	0
Boston Red Sox	96	59	.619	I
New York Yankees	94	60	.610	2-1/2
Philadelphia Athletics	84	70	.545	12-1/2
Detroit Tigers	78	76	.506	18-1/2
St. Louis Browns	59	94	.386	37
Washington Senators	56	97	.366	40
Chicago White Sox	51	101	.336	44-1/2

In 1948, for the first time in American League history, the season ended in a tie between the Cleveland Indians and the Boston Red Sox. In a one-game playoff, the Cleveland Indians beat the Boston Red Sox by a score of 8-3 to take the American League championship. The Indians went on to win the 1948 World Series by beating the Boston Braves four games to two.

Another first in 1948 was the first no-hitter thrown under the lights by Bob Lemon of the Cleveland Indians on June 30 at Briggs Stadium. Cleveland won the game 2-0 over Detroit.

In 1948, the Cleveland Indians were accused of pulling a publicity stunt by signing a 42-year old all-time great veteran pitcher from the Negro League to a Major League contract. Satchel Paige went on to pitch his way to a 6-1 season as the oldest player to ever debut in the majors. His first appearance in relief of pitcher Bob Lemon, on July 9, made him the first black pitcher in American League history. This was also the first time in World Series history a black player took the mound.

1948 TEAM LEADING HITTING STATISTICS

Statistic	Team	#
Base on Balls	Boston	823
Batting Average	Cleveland	.282
Doubles	Boston	277
Hits	Cleveland	1,534
Home Runs	Cleveland	155
On Base Percentage	Boston	.374
Runs	Boston	907
Slugging Average	New York	.432
Stolen Bases	Washington	76
Triples	New York	75
	Washington	

1948 TEAM LEADING PITCHING STATISTICS

Statistic	Team	#
Complete Games	Philadelphia	74
ERA	Cleveland	.323
Fewest Hits Allowed	Cleveland	1,246
Fewest Home Runs Allowed	Washington	81
Fewest Walks Allowed	Detroit	589
Saves	Cleveland	30
Shutouts	Cleveland	26
Strikeouts	Detroit	678

1948 INDIVIDUAL LEADING HITTING STATISTICS

Statistic	Name(s)	Team	#
Base on Balls	Ted Williams	Boston	126
Batting Average	Ted Williams	Boston	.369
Doubles	Ted Williams	Boston	44
Hits	Bob Dillinger	St. Louis	207
Home Runs	Joe DiMaggio	New York	39
On Base Percentage	Ted Williams	Boston	.497
RBI	Joe DiMaggio	New York	155
Runs	Tommy Henrich	New York	138
Slugging Average	Ted Williams	Boston	.615
Stolen Bases	Bob Dilllinger	St. Louis	28
Total Bases	Joe DiMaggio	New York	355
Triples	Tommy Henrich	New York	14

1948 INDIVIDUAL LEADING PITCHING STATISTICS

Statistic	Name(s)	Team	#
Complete Games	Bob Lemon	Cleveland	20
ERA	Gene Bearden	Cleveland	2.43
Games	Joe Page	New York	55
Saves	Russ Christopher	Cleveland	17
Shutouts	Bob Lemon	Cleveland	10
Strikeouts	Bob Feller	Cleveland	164
Winning Percentage	Jack Kramer	Boston	.783
Wins	Hal Newhouser	Detroit	21

* * * * *

CLEVELAND INDIANS NOTES

Ballpark: Cleveland Stadium
Manager/Player: Lou Boudreau
Runs Scored: 840
Runs Allowed: 568
Total Attendance: 2,620,627

TEAM BATTING

Pos		Player	AG	G	AB	R	H	2B	3B	HR	RBI	BB	SO	BA
C		Jim Hegan	27	144	472	60	117	21	6	14	61	48	74	.248
1B	*	Eddie Robinson	27	134	493	53	125	18	5	16	83	36	42	.254
2B		Joe Gordon	33	144	550	96	154	21	4	32	124	77	68	.280
3B		Ken Keltner	31	153	558	91	166	24	4	31	119	89	52	.297
SS		Lou Boudreau	30	152	560	116	199	34	6	18	106	98	9	.355
OF	*	Dale Mitchell	26	141	608	82	204	30	8	4	56	45	17	.336
OF	*	Larry Doby	24	121	439	83	132	23	9	14	66	54	77	.301
OF	*	Thurman Tucker	30	83	242	52	63	13	2	1	19	31	17	.260

Pos		Player	AG	G	AB	R	H	2B	3B	HR	RBI	BB	SO	BA
		Allie Clark	25	81	271	43	84	5	2	9	38	23	13	.310
	*	Wally Judnich	31	79	218	36	56	13	3	2	29	56	23	.257
	*	Hank Edwards	29	55	160	27	43	9	2	3	18	18	18	.269
		Johnny Berardino	31	66	147	19	28	5	1	2	10	27	16	.190
		Joe Tipton	26	47	90	11	26	3	0	1	13	4	10	.289
		Bob Kennedy	27	66	73	10	22	3	2	0	5	4	6	.301
	*	Hal Peck	31	45	63	12	18	3	0	0	8	4	8	.286
		Pat Seerey	25	10	23	7	6	0	0	1	6	7	8	.261
		Ray Boone	24	6	5	0	2	1	0	0	1	0	1	.400
		Al Rosen	24	5	5	0	1	0	0	0	0	0	2	.200
		Ray Murray	30	4	4	0	0	0	0	0	0	0	3	.000
	*	Bob Lemon	27	52	119	20	34	9	0	5	21	8	23	.286
		Bob Feller	29	44	95	1	9	2	0	0	3	1	39	.095
	*	Gene Bearden	27	37	90	14	23	3	0	2	14	5	9	.256
	#	Steve Gromek	28	38	41	3	6	1	0	0	1	3	7	.146
	*	Sam Zoldak	29	23	36	0	5	1	0	0	0	1	6	.139
		Satchel Paige	41	21	23	0	2	0	0	0	0	0	5	.087
		Bob Muncrief	32	21	18	0	2	0	0	0	0	2	6	.111
		Don Black	31	18	15	1	3	0	0	0	0	0	3	.200
		Ed Klieman	30	44	14	0	2	0	0	0	0	2	9	.143
		Russ Christopher	30	45	6	1	0	0	0	0	0	0	2	3	.000
		Al Gettel	30	5	3	1	0	0	0	0	0	0	0	.000
	*	Bill Kennedy	27	6	3	1	2	0	0	0	0	1	0	.667
		Lyman Linde	27	3	2	0	0	0	0	0	0	0	1	.000

TEAM PITCHING

Pos		Player	AG	G	ERA	W	L	SV	CG	IP	H	R	ER	BB	HR	SO
SP		Bob Feller	29	44	3.56	19	15	3	18	280.3	255	123	111	116	20	164
SP		Bob Lemon	27	43	2.82	20	14	2	20	293.7	231	104	92	129	12	147
SP	*	Gene Bearden	27	37	2.43	20	7	1	15	229.7	187	72	62	106	9	80

Pos		Player	AG	G	ERA	W	L	SV	CG	IP	H	R	ER	BB	HR	SO
SP	*	Sam Zoldak	29	23	2.81	9	6	0	4	105.7	104	37	33	24	6	17
SP		Don Black	31	18	5.37	2	2	0	1	52.0	57	33	31	40	5	16
CL		Russ Christopher	30	45	2.90	3	2	17	0	59.0	55	21	19	27	3	14
RP		Ed Klieman	30	44	2.60	3	2	4	0	79.7	62	26	23	46	3	18
RP		Steve Gromek	28	38	2.84	9	3	2	4	130.0	109	52	41	51	10	50
RP		Satchel Paige	41	21	2.48	6	1	1	3	72.7	61	21	20	25	2	45
RP		Bob Muncrief	32	21	3.98	5	4	0	1	72.3	76	37	32	31	8	24
	*	Bill Kennedy	27	6	11.12	1	0	0	0	11.3	16	14	14	13	0	12
		Lyman Linde	27	3	5.40	0	0	0	0	10.0	9	6	6	4	1	0
		Al Gettel	30	5	17.61	0	1	0	0	7.7	15	15	15	10	2	4
		Mike Garcia	24	1	0.00	0	0	0	0	2.0	3	0	0	0	0	1
		Butch Wensloff	32	1	10.80	0	1	0	0	1.7	2	2	2	3	1	2
		Ernest Groth	26	1	9.00	0	0	0	0	1.0	1	1	1	2	0	0
		Les Webber	33	1	40.50	0	0	0	0	0.7	3	3	3	1	0	1

* * * * *

BOSTON RED SOX NOTES

Ballpark:	Fenway Park
Manager:	Joe McCarthy
Runs Scored:	907
Runs Allowed:	720
Total Attendance:	1,558,798

TEAM BATTING

Pos		Player	AG	G	AB	R	H	2B	3B	HR	RBI	BB	SO	BA
C		Birdie Tebbetts	35	128	446	54	125	26	2	5	68	62	32	.280
1B	*	Billy Goodman	22	127	445	65	138	27	2	1	66	74	44	.310
2B		Bobby Doerr	30	140	527	94	150	23	6	27	111	83	49	.285
3B	*	Johnny Pesky	28	143	565	124	159	26	6	3	55	99	32	.281

Pos		Player	AG	G	AB	R	H	2B	3B	HR	RBI	BB	SO	BA
SS		Vern Stephens	27	155	635	114	171	25	8	29	137	77	56	.269
OF		Dom DiMaggio	31	155	648	127	185	40	4	9	87	101	58	.285
OF	*	Ted Williams	29	137	509	124	188	44	3	25	127	126	41	.369
OF	*	Stan Spence	33	114	391	71	92	17	4	12	61	82	33	.235
	*	Wally Moses	37	78	189	26	49	12	1	2	29	21	19	.259
		Sam Mele	25	66	180	25	42	12	1	2	25	13	21	.233
		Billy Hitchcock	31	49	124	15	37	3	2	1	20	7	9	.298
		Matt Batts	26	46	118	13	37	12	0	1	24	15	9	.314
		Jake Jones	27	36	105	3	21	4	0	1	8	11	26	.200
		Lou Stringer	31	4	11	1	1	0	0	1	1	0	3	.091
		Babe Martin	28	4	4	0	2	0	0	0	0	0	1	.500
	*	Tom Wright	24	3	2	1	1	0	1	0	0	0	0	.500
		Johnny Ostrowski	30	1	1	0	0	0	0	0	0	0	1	.000
		Neill Sheridan	26	2	1	0	0	0	0	0	0	0	1	.000
		Joe Dobson	31	38	84	9	17	2	0	1	4	6	27	.202
	*	Mel Parnell	26	35	80	6	13	1	0	0	8	1	11	.162
		Jack Kramer	30	29	73	7	11	1	0	1	8	10	21	.151
		Ellis Kinder	33	28	62	8	6	0	0	0	4	8	18	.097
		Denny Galehouse	36	27	42	6	7	0	0	0	1	8	13	.167
	*	Dave Ferriss	26	31	37	4	9	1	0	0	6	6	6	.243
	*	Mickey Harris	31	20	32	6	2	0	0	0	1	10	6	.062
	*	Earl Johnson	29	35	31	2	3	0	0	0	3	1	9	.097
	*	Mickey McDermott	19	7	8	2	3	1	0	0	0	0	0	.375
		Harry Dorish	26	9	4	0	1	0	0	0	0	0	1	.250
		Earl Caldwell	43	8	3	0	1	0	0	0	0	0	1	.333
		Mike Palm	23	3	3	0	0	0	0	0	0	0	1	.000
		Tex Hughson	32	15	2	0	0	0	0	0	0	0	0	.000
	*	Chuck Stobbs	18	6	1	0	0	0	0	0	0	0	0	.000

TEAM PITCHING

Pos		Player	AG	G	ERA	W	L	SV	CG	IP	H	R	ER	BB	HR	SO
SP		Joe Dobson	31	38	3.56	16	10	2	16	245.3	237	115	97	92	14	116
SP		Jack Kramer	30	29	4.35	18	5	0	14	205.0	233	104	99	64	12	72
SP	*	Mel Parnell	26	35	3.14	15	8	0	16	212.0	205	87	74	90	7	77
SP		Ellis Kinder	33	28	3.74	10	7	0	10	178.0	183	84	74	63	10	53
SP	*	Mickey Harris	31	20	5.30	7	10	0	6	113.7	120	73	67	59	10	42
SP		Denny Galehouse	36	27	4.00	8	8	3	6	137.3	152	68	61	46	10	38
CL	*	Earl Johnson	29	35	4.53	10	4	5	1	91.3	98	49	46	42	7	45
RP		Dave Ferriss	26	31	5.23	7	3	3	1	115.3	127	71	67	61	7	30
RP		Tex Hughson	32	15	5.12	3	1	0	0	19.3	21	14	11	7	0	6
	*	Mickey McDermott	19	7	6.17	0	0	0	0	23.3	16	18	16	35	2	17
		Harry Dorish	26	9	5.65	0	1	0	0	14.3	18	13	9	6	1	5
		Earl Caldwell	43	8	13.00	1	1	0	0	9.0	11	14	13	11	2	5
	*	Chuck Stobbs	18	6	6.43	0	0	0	0	7.0	9	5	5	7	0	4
		Cot Deal	25	4	0.00	1	0	0	0	4.0	3	0	0	3	0	2
		Mike Palm	23	3	6.00	0	0	0	0	3.0	6	2	2	5	0	1
	*	Windy McCall	22	1	20.25	0	1	0	0	1.3	6	3	3	1	1	0

* * * * *

NEW YORK YANKEES NOTES

Ballpark:	Yankee Stadium
Manager:	Bucky Harris
Runs Scored:	857
Runs Allowed:	633
Total Attendance:	2,373,901

TEAM BATTING

Pos		Player	AG	G	AB	R	H	2B	3B	HR	RBI	BB	SO	BA
C		Gus Niarhos	27	83	228	41	61	12	2	0	19	52	15	.268
1B	*	George McQuinn	38	94	302	33	75	11	4	11	41	40	38	.248
2B		Snuffy Stirnweiss	29	141	515	90	130	20	7	3	32	86	62	.252
3B		Billy Johnson	29	127	446	59	131	20	6	12	64	41	30	.294
SS		Phil Rizzuto	30	128	464	65	117	13	2	6	50	60	24	.252
OF		Joe DiMaggio	33	153	594	110	190	26	11	39	155	67	30	.320
OF	*	Tommy Henrich	35	146	588	138	181	42	14	25	100	76	42	.308
OF		Johnny Lindell	31	88	309	58	98	17	2	13	55	35	50	.317
	*	Yogi Berra	23	125	469	70	143	24	10	14	98	25	24	.305
	*	Bobby Brown	23	113	363	62	109	19	5	3	48	48	16	.300
	*	Charlie Keller	31	83	247	41	66	15	2	6	44	41	25	.267
		Steve Souchock	29	44	118	11	24	3	1	3	11	7	13	.203
	*	Cliff Mapes	26	53	88	19	22	11	1	1	12	6	13	.250
		Hank Bauer	25	19	50	6	9	1	1	1	9	6	13	.180
		Sherm Lollar	23	22	38	0	8	0	0	0	4	1	6	.211
		Ralph Houk	28	14	29	3	8	2	0	0	3	0	6	.276
		Frankie Crosetti	37	17	14	4	4	0	1	0	0	2	0	.286
		Charlie Silvera	23	4	14	1	8	0	1	0	1	0	1	.571
	*	Joe Collins	25	5	5	0	1	1	0	0	2	0	1	.200
	*	Bud Stewart	32	6	5	1	1	1	0	0	0	0	0	.200
		Jack Phillips	26	1	2	0	0	0	0	0	0	0	1	.000
	*	Lonny Frey	37	1	0	1	0	0	0	0	0	0	0	.000
		Allie Reynolds	31	41	83	6	16	3	0	1	16	4	22	.193
	*	Ed Lopat	30	34	81	6	14	0	0	0	10	8	6	.173
		Vic Raschi	29	36	81	10	19	4	0	0	11	5	11	.235
		Spec Shea	27	28	47	4	7	0	2	0	4	6	11	.149
	*	Tommy Byrne	28	31	46	8	15	3	1	1	7	1	7	.326
		Red Embree	30	20	27	2	4	1	0	0	3	1	6	.148
	*	Joe Page	30	55	24	3	7	1	2	0	2	3	4	.292

Pos	Player	AG	G	AB	R	H	2B	3B	HR	RBI	BB	SO	BA
	Bob Porterfield	24	16	24	4	6	0	0	0	1	1	4	.250
	Frank Hiller	27	22	16	1	6	1	0	0	4	0	2	.375
	Karl Drews	28	19	7	0	0	0	0	0	0	1	1	.000

TEAM PITCHING

Pos		Player	AG	G	ERA	W	L	SV	CG	IP	H	R	ER	BB	HR	SO
SP	*	Ed Lopat	30	33	3.65	17	11	0	13	226.7	246	106	92	66	16	83
SP		Vic Raschi	29	36	3.84	19	8	1	18	222.7	208	103	95	74	15	124
SP		Allie Reynolds	31	39	3.77	16	7	3	11	236.3	240	108	99	111	17	101
SP		Spec Shea	27	28	3.41	9	10	1	8	155.7	117	66	59	87	10	71
SP		Bob Porterfield	24	16	4.50	5	3	0	2	78.0	85	42	39	34	5	30
CL	*	Joe Page	30	55	4.26	7	8	16	0	107.7	116	59	51	66	6	77
RP	*	Tommy Byrne	28	31	3.30	8	5	2	5	133.7	79	55	49	101	8	93
RP		Karl Drews	28	19	3.79	2	3	1	0	38.0	35	17	16	31	3	11
RP		Frank Hiller	27	22	4.04	5	2	0	1	62.3	59	29	28	30	8	25
RP		Randy Gumpert	30	15	2.88	1	0	0	0	25.0	27	10	8	6	0	12
		Red Embree	30	20	3.76	5	3	0	4	76.7	77	37	32	30	6	25
		Dick Starr	27	1	4.50	0	0	0	0	2.0	0	1	1	2	0	2
		Cuddles Marshall	23	1	0.00	0	0	0	0	1.0	0	0	0	3	0	0

* * * * *

PHILADELPHIA ATHLETICS NOTES

Ballpark:	Shibe Park
Manager:	Connie Mack
Runs Scored:	729
Runs Allowed:	735
Total Attendance:	945,076

TEAM BATTING

Pos		Player	AG	G	AB	R	H	2B	3B	HR	RBI	BB	SO	BA
C		Buddy Rosar	33	90	302	30	77	13	0	4	41	39	12	.255
1B	*	Ferris Fain	27	145	520	81	146	27	6	7	88	113	37	.281
2B		Pete Suder	32	148	519	64	125	23	5	7	60	60	60	.241
3B		Hank Majeski	31	148	590	88	183	41	4	12	120	48	43	.310
SS		Eddie Joost	32	135	509	99	127	22	2	16	55	119	87	.250
OF	*	Barney McCosky	31	135	515	95	168	21	5	0	46	68	22	.326
OF		Sam Chapman	32	123	445	58	115	18	6	13	70	55	50	.258
OF	*	Elmer Valo	27	113	383	72	117	17	4	3	46	81	13	.305
		Don White	29	86	253	29	62	14	2	1	28	19	16	.245
	*	Ray Coleman	26	68	210	32	51	6	6	0	21	31	17	.243
		Mike Guerra	35	53	142	18	30	4	2	1	23	18	13	.211
	*	Herman Franks	34	40	98	10	22	7	1	1	14	16	11	.224
		Skeeter Webb	38	23	54	5	8	2	0	0	3	0	9	.148
		Rudy York	34	31	51	4	8	0	0	0	6	7	15	.157
	*	George Binks	31	17	41	2	4	1	0	0	2	2	2	.098
		Billy DeMars	22	18	29	3	5	0	0	0	1	5	3	.172
	*	Nellie Fox	20	3	13	0	2	0	0	0	0	1	0	.154
		Bob Wellman	22	4	10	1	2	0	1	0	0	3	2	.200
	*	Earle Brucker	22	2	6	0	1	1	0	0	0	1	1	.167
		Carl Scheib	21	52	104	14	31	8	3	2	21	8	17	.298
		Dick Fowler	27	29	82	5	14	1	0	1	8	3	10	.171
	*	Lou Brissie	24	39	76	3	18	1	0	0	10	2	8	.237
		Joe Coleman	25	33	74	2	9	2	0	0	7	5	29	.122
		Phil Marchildon	34	33	72	3	5	0	0	0	2	10	30	.069
		Bill McCahan	27	17	31	4	8	1	0	0	8	2	2	.258
		Bubba Harris	22	45	24	4	3	0	0	0	1	3	5	.125
		Bob Savage	26	33	13	2	1	0	0	0	0	3	6	.077
		Alex Kellner	23	13	5	0	0	0	0	0	0	0	1	.000
		Wally Holborow	34	5	4	1	2	1	0	0	3	1	1	.500

Pos		Player	AG	G	AB	R	H	2B	3B	HR	RBI	BB	SO	BA
	*	Nels Potter	36	8	4	0	I	0	0	0	0	I	0	.250
		Bill Dietrich	38	4	2	0	0	0	0	0	0	I	I	.000

TEAM PITCHING

Pos		Player	AG	G	ERA	W	L	SV	CG	IP	H	R	ER	BB	HR	SO
SP		Phil Marchildon	34	33	4.53	9	15	0	12	226.3	214	133	114	131	19	66
SP		Joe Coleman	25	33	4.09	14	13	0	13	215.7	224	105	98	90	11	86
SP		Dick Fowler	27	29	3.78	15	8	2	16	204.7	221	93	86	76	15	50
SP	*	Lou Brissie	24	39	4.13	14	10	5	11	194.0	202	100	89	95	6	127
SP		Carl Scheib	21	32	3.94	14	8	0	15	198.7	219	90	87	76	14	44
SP		Bill McCahan	27	17	5.71	4	7	0	5	86.7	98	58	55	65	8	20
CL		Bubba Harris	22	45	4.13	5	2	5	0	93.7	89	51	43	35	2	32
RP		Bob Savage	26	33	6.21	5	I	5	I	75.3	98	55	52	33	9	26
RP	*	Alex Kellner	23	13	7.83	0	0	0	0	23.0	21	20	20	16	0	14
		Nels Potter	36	8	4.00	2	2	I	0	18.0	17	8	8	5	I	13
		Wally Holborow	34	5	5.71	I	2	0	I	17.3	32	12	11	7	I	3
		Bill Dietrich	38	4	5.87	I	2	0	0	15.3	21	10	10	9	0	5

* * * * *

DETROIT TIGERS NOTES

Ballpark: Briggs Stadium
Manager: Steve O'Neill
Runs Scored: 700
Runs Allowed: 726
Total Attendance: 1,743,035

TEAM BATTING

Pos		Player	AG	G	AB	R	H	2B	3B	HR	RBI	BB	SO	BA
C		Bob Swift	33	113	292	23	65	6	0	4	66	51	29	.223
1B	*	George Vico	24	144	521	50	139	23	9	8	58	39	39	.267
2B	*	Eddie Mayo	38	106	370	35	92	20	1	2	42	30	19	.249
3B		George Kell	25	92	368	47	112	24	3	2	44	33	15	.304
SS		Johnny Lipon	25	121	458	65	133	18	8	5	52	68	22	.290
OF		Hoot Evers	27	139	538	81	169	33	6	10	103	51	31	.314
OF	*	Pat Mullin	30	138	496	91	143	16	11	23	80	77	57	.288
OF	*	Vic Wertz	23	119	391	49	97	19	9	7	67	48	70	.248
	*	Dick Wakefield	27	110	322	50	89	20	5	11	53	70	55	.276
		Neil Berry	26	87	256	46	68	8	1	0	16	37	23	.266
		Eddie Lake	32	64	198	51	52	6	0	2	18	57	20	.263
		Jimmy Outlaw	35	74	198	33	56	12	0	0	25	31	15	.283
	*	Hal Wagner	32	54	109	10	22	3	0	0	10	20	11	.202
	*	Paul Campbell	30	59	83	15	22	1	1	1	11	1	10	.265
		Hank Riebe	26	25	62	0	12	0	0	0	5	3	5	.194
	*	Joe Ginsberg	21	11	36	7	13	0	0	0	1	3	1	.361
		Johnny Groth	21	6	17	3	8	3	0	1	5	1	1	.471
	*	Johnny Bero	25	4	9	2	0	0	0	0	0	1	1	.000
		Ed Mierkowicz	24	3	5	0	1	0	0	0	1	2	2	.200
	*	Doc Cramer	42	4	4	1	0	0	0	0	1	3	0	.000
	*	John McHale	26	1	1	0	0	0	0	0	0	0	0	.000
	*	Fred Hutchinson	28	76	112	11	23	1	0	1	12	22	0	.205
	*	Hal Newhouser	27	39	92	6	19	0	1	0	6	10	14	.207
		Virgil Trucks	31	43	79	6	13	0	1	0	2	2	14	.165
		Dizzy Trout	33	32	69	6	15	3	0	1	2	5	14	.217
		Art Houtteman	20	43	56	2	11	0	0	0	7	0	2	.196
	#	Ted Gray	23	26	29	2	7	1	0	0	1	2	7	.241
	*	Billy Pierce	21	22	17	5	5	0	2	0	2	0	4	.294
		Stubby Overmire	29	37	14	0	1	0	0	0	1	2	1	.071

Pos	Player	AG	G	AB	R	H	2B	3B	HR	RBI	BB	SO	BA
	Hal White	29	27	13	1	2	1	0	0	1	2	6	.154
	Al Benton	37	30	11	1	2	1	0	0	1	0	6	.182
	Lou Kretlow	27	5	8	0	4	0	0	0	1	0	1	.500
	Rufe Gentry	30	4	1	1	1	0	0	0	0	0	0	1.000

TEAM PITCHING

Pos		Player	AG	G	ERA	W	L	SV	CG	IP	H	R	ER	BB	HR	SO
SP	*	Hal Newhouser	27	39	3.01	21	12	1	19	272.3	249	109	91	99	10	143
SP		Fred Hutchinson	28	33	4.32	13	11	0	15	221.0	223	119	106	48	32	92
SP		Virgil Trucks	31	43	3.78	14	13	2	7	211.7	190	97	89	85	14	123
SP		Dizzy Trout	33	32	3.43	10	14	2	11	183.7	193	87	70	73	6	91
CL		Art Houtteman	20	43	4.66	2	16	10	4	164.3	186	101	85	52	11	74
RP	*	Stubby Overmire	29	37	5.97	3	4	3	0	66.3	89	48	44	31	5	14
RP		Al Benton	37	30	5.68	2	2	3	0	44.3	45	34	28	36	4	18
RP		Hal White	29	27	6.12	2	1	1	0	42.7	46	31	29	26	2	17
RP	*	Billy Pierce	21	22	6.34	3	0	0	0	55.3	47	40	39	51	5	36
	*	Ted Gray	23	26	4.22	6	2	0	3	85.3	73	43	40	72	2	60
		Lou Kretlow	27	5	4.63	2	1	0	1	23.3	21	14	12	11	1	9
		Rufe Gentry	30	4	2.70	0	0	0	0	6.7	5	2	2	5	0	1

* * * * *

ST. LOUIS BROWNS NOTES

Ballpark: Sportsman's Park
Manager: Zack Taylor
Runs Scored: 671
Runs Allowed: 849
Total Attendance: 335,564

TEAM BATTING

Pos		Player	AG	G	AB	R	H	2B	3B	HR	RBI	BB	SO	BA
C		Les Moss	23	107	335	35	86	12	1	14	46	39	50	.257
1B	#	Chuck Stevens	29	85	287	34	75	12	4	1	26	41	26	.261
2B		Jerry Priddy	28	151	560	96	166	40	9	8	79	86	71	.296
3B		Bob Dillinger	29	153	644	110	207	34	10	2	44	65	34	.321
SS		Eddie Pellagrini	30	105	290	31	69	8	3	2	27	34	40	.238
OF	*	Al Zarilla	29	144	529	77	174	39	3	12	74	48	48	.329
OF		Whitey Platt	27	123	454	57	123	22	10	7	82	39	51	.271
OF	*	Paul Lehner	27	103	333	23	92	15	4	2	46	30	19	.276
		Sam Dente	26	98	267	26	72	11	2	0	22	22	8	.270
	*	Dick Kokos	20	71	258	40	77	15	3	4	40	28	32	.298
	*	Hank Arft	26	69	248	25	59	10	3	5	38	45	43	.238
		Roy Partee	30	82	231	14	47	8	1	0	17	25	21	.203
		Don Lund	25	63	161	21	40	7	4	3	25	10	17	.248
		Pete Laydon	28	41	104	11	26	2	1	0	4	6	10	.250
		Andy Anderson	25	51	87	13	24	5	1	1	12	8	15	.276
	*	Joe Schultz	29	43	37	0	7	0	0	0	9	6	3	.189
	*	Ray Coleman	26	17	29	2	5	0	1	0	2	2	5	.172
		Ken Wood	23	10	24	2	2	0	1	0	2	1	4	.083
	*	George Binks	31	15	23	2	5	0	0	0	1	2	1	.217
	*	Jerry McCarthy	25	2	3	0	1	0	0	0	0	0	0	.333
		Tom Jordan	28	1	1	0	0	0	0	0	0	0	0	.000
	#	Fred Sanford	28	43	73	9	11	3	0	1	4	4	17	.151
		Ned Garver	22	46	66	9	19	1	1	1	9	4	3	.288
	*	Cliff Fannin	24	48	65	12	11	0	0	0	2	11	4	.169
	*	Bill Kennedy	27	26	44	5	11	1	0	0	4	3	4	.250
		Bryan Stephens	27	43	32	4	4	1	0	0	3	6	9	.125
	*	Frank Biscan	28	47	26	3	5	2	0	0	2	4	7	.192
	*	Sam Zoldak	29	11	22	3	6	1	0	0	2	0	3	.273
	*	Joe Ostrowski	31	26	18	2	4	0	0	0	2	4	5	.222

Pos		Player	AG	G	AB	R	H	2B	3B	HR	RBI	BB	SO	BA
		Blackie Schwamb	21	12	10	1	3	1	0	0	0	1	2	.300
		Al Widmar	23	49	10	1	3	1	0	0	0	1	4	.300
		Ray Shore	27	17	9	0	0	0	0	0	0	0	3	.000
		Karl Drews	28	20	8	2	0	0	0	0	0	3	6	.000
	*	Al Gerheauser	31	14	6	0	2	0	0	0	0	0	2	.333
	*	Clem Dreisewerd	32	13	5	0	0	0	0	0	0	0	4	.000
	*	Nels Potter	36	2	4	1	2	0	0	0	1	0	0	.500

TEAM PITCHING

Pos		Player	AG	G	ERA	W	L	SV	CG	IP	H	R	ER	BB	HR	SO
SP		Fred Sanford	28	42	4.64	12	21	2	9	227.0	250	123	117	91	19	79
SP		Cliff Fannin	24	34	4.17	10	14	1	10	213.7	198	106	99	104	14	102
SP		Ned Garver	22	38	3.41	7	11	5	7	198.0	200	92	75	95	14	75
SP	*	Bill Kennedy	27	26	4.70	7	8	0	3	132.0	132	82	69	104	10	77
RP		Al Widmar	23	49	4.46	2	6	1	0	82.7	88	42	41	48	4	34
RP	*	Frank Biscan	28	47	6.11	6	7	2	1	98.7	129	78	67	71	3	45
RP		Bryan Stephens	27	43	6.02	3	6	3	2	122.7	141	94	82	67	14	35
RP		Karl Drews	28	20	8.05	3	2	2	0	38.0	43	35	34	38	3	11
	*	Joe Ostrowski	31	26	5.97	4	6	3	3	78.3	108	54	52	17	6	20
	*	Sam Zoldak	29	11	4.67	2	4	0	0	54.0	64	30	28	19	4	13
		Ray Shore	27	17	6.39	1	2	0	0	38.0	40	30	27	35	2	12
		Blackie Schwamb	21	12	8.53	1	1	0	0	31.7	44	34	30	21	3	7
	*	Al Gerheauser	31	14	7.33	0	3	0	0	23.3	32	23	19	10	0	10
	*	Clem Dreisewerd	32	13	5.64	0	2	1	0	22.3	28	15	14	8	6	6
		Nels Potter	36	2	5.23	1	1	0	0	10.3	11	7	6	4	1	4
		Jim Wilson	26	4	13.50	0	0	0	0	2.7	5	4	4	5	0	1

* * * * *

WASHINGTON SENATORS NOTES

Ballpark:	Griffith Stadium
Manager:	Joe Kuhel
Runs Scored:	578
Runs Allowed:	796
Total Attendance:	795,254

TEAM BATTING

Pos		Player	AG	G	AB	R	H	2B	3B	HR	RBI	BB	SO	BA
C	*	Jake Early	33	97	246	22	54	7	2	1	28	36	33	.220
1B	*	Mickey Vernon	30	150	558	78	135	27	7	3	48	54	43	.242
2B		Al Kozar	26	150	577	61	144	25	8	1	58	66	52	.250
3B		Eddie Yost	21	145	555	74	138	32	11	2	50	82	51	.249
SS		Mark Christman	34	120	409	38	106	17	2	1	40	25	19	.259
OF	*	Gil Coan	26	138	513	56	119	13	9	7	60	41	78	.232
OF	*	Bud Stewart	32	118	401	56	112	17	13	7	69	49	27	.279
OF		Junior Wooten	24	88	258	34	66	8	3	1	23	24	21	.256
		Al Evans	31	93	228	19	59	6	3	2	28	38	20	.259
		Carden Gillenwater	30	77	221	23	54	10	4	3	21	39	36	.244
		Tom McBride	33	92	206	22	53	9	1	1	29	28	15	.257
	*	Sherry Robertson	29	71	187	19	46	11	3	2	22	24	26	.246
		John Sullivan	27	85	173	25	36	4	1	0	12	22	25	.208
		Len Okrie	24	19	42	1	10	0	1	0	1	1	7	.238
		Sammy Meeks	25	24	33	4	4	1	0	0	2	1	12	.121
		Leon Culberson	28	12	29	1	5	0	0	0	2	8	5	.172
		Angel Fleitas	33	15	13	1	1	0	0	0	1	3	5	.077
		Jim Clark	20	9	12	1	3	0	0	0	0	0	2	.250
	*	Larry Drake	27	4	7	0	2	0	0	0	1	1	3	.286
		Clyde Vollmer	26	1	5	1	2	0	0	0	0	0	1	.400
		Jay Difani	24	2	2	0	0	0	0	0	0	0	2	.000

Pos		Player	AG	G	AB	R	H	2B	3B	HR	RBI	BB	SO	BA
	#	Early Wynn	28	73	106	9	23	3	1	0	16	14	22	.217
		Ray Scarborough	30	31	64	7	14	3	1	0	9	0	8	.219
		Sid Hudson	33	39	59	5	14	4	1	0	4	3	6	.237
		Walt Masterson	28	33	57	8	11	2	1	0	4	2	22	.193
	*	Mickey Haefner	35	28	43	1	7	1	0	0	3	3	9	.163
	*	Forrest Thompson	30	46	35	4	10	2	1	0	4	2	4	.286
		Milo Candini	30	35	22	3	8	1	0	0	0	3	2	.364
		Earl Harrist	28	23	18	1	3	0	0	0	0	0	6	.167
		Tom Ferrick	33	37	15	1	1	0	1	0	1	0	3	.067
		Dick Welteroth	20	33	10	1	1	0	0	0	0	0	4	.100
		Dick Weik	20	3	4	1	3	0	1	0	0	0	0	.750
		Marino Pieretti	27	13	2	1	0	0	0	0	1	0	1	.000
		Ramon Garcia	24	4	1	0	1	0	0	0	0	0	0	1.000

TEAM PITCHING

Pos		Player	AG	G	ERA	W	L	SV	CG	IP	H	R	ER	BB	HR	SO
SP		Early Wynn	28	33	5.82	8	19	0	15	198.0	236	144	128	94	18	49
SP		Sid Hudson	33	39	5.88	4	16	1	4	182.0	217	128	119	107	11	53
SP		Walt Masterson	28	33	3.83	8	15	2	9	188.0	171	88	80	122	12	72
SP		Ray Scarborough	30	31	2.82	15	8	1	9	185.3	166	71	58	72	10	76
SP	*	Mickey Haefner	35	28	4.02	5	13	0	4	147.7	151	86	66	61	7	45
CL		Tom Ferrick	33	37	4.15	2	5	10	0	73.7	75	37	34	38	3	34
RP	*	Forrest Thompson	30	46	3.84	6	10	4	0	131.3	134	71	56	54	9	40
RP		Milo Candini	30	35	5.15	2	3	3	1	94.3	96	56	54	63	1	23
RP		Dick Welteroth	20	33	5.51	2	1	1	0	65.3	73	43	40	50	6	16
RP		Earl Harrist	28	23	4.60	3	3	0	0	60.7	70	35	31	37	1	21
		Dick Weik	20	3	5.68	1	2	0	0	12.7	14	8	8	22	1	8
		Marino Pieretti	27	8	10.80	0	2	0	0	11.7	18	14	17	7	1	6
		Ramon Garcia	24	4	17.18	0	0	0	0	3.7	11	7	7	4	0	2

Pos		Player	AG	G	ERA	W	L	SV	CG	IP	H	R	ER	BB	HR	SO
	*	Junior Wooten	24	1	9.00	0	0	0	0	2.0	2	2	2	2	0	1
		Cal Cooper	25	1	45.00	0	0	0	0	1.0	5	5	5	1	1	0

* * * * *

CHICAGO WHITE SOX NOTES

Ballpark: Comiskey Park
Manager: Ted Lyons
Runs Scored: 559
Runs Allowed: 814
Total Attendance: 777,844

TEAM BATTING

Pos		Player	AG	G	AB	R	H	2B	3B	HR	RBI	BB	SO	BA
C	*	Aaron Robinson	33	98	326	47	82	14	2	8	39	46	30	.252
1B	*	Tony Lupien	31	154	617	69	152	19	3	6	54	74	38	.246
2B		Don Kolloway	29	119	417	60	114	14	4	6	38	18	18	.273
3B		Luke Appling	41	139	497	63	156	16	2	0	47	94	35	.314
SS		Cass Michaels	22	145	484	47	120	12	6	5	56	69	42	.248
OF	#	Dave Philley	28	137	488	51	140	28	3	5	42	50	33	.287
OF	*	Taffy Wright	36	134	455	50	127	15	6	4	61	38	18	.279
OF		Pat Seerey	25	95	340	44	78	11	0	18	64	61	94	.229
	*	Floyd Baker	31	104	335	47	72	8	3	0	18	73	26	.215
	*	Ralph Hodgin	32	114	331	28	88	11	5	1	34	21	11	.266
		Ralph Weigel	26	66	163	8	38	7	3	0	26	13	18	.233
		Bob Kennedy	27	30	113	4	28	8	1	0	14	4	17	.248
		Mike Tresh	34	39	108	10	27	1	0	1	11	9	9	.250
	*	Jim Delsing	22	20	63	5	12	0	0	0	5	5	12	.190
	#	Jack Wallaesa	28	33	48	2	9	0	0	1	3	1	12	.187
	*	Herb Adams	20	5	11	1	3	1	0	0	0	1	1	.273

Pos		Player	AG	G	AB	R	H	2B	3B	HR	RBI	BB	SO	BA
	*	Jerry Scala	23	3	6	1	0	0	0	0	0	0	3	.000
		Frank Whitman	23	3	6	0	0	0	0	0	0	0	3	.000
	*	Bill Wight	26	34	73	2	6	0	0	0	3	3	31	.082
		Al Gettel	30	24	54	4	13	2	0	0	3	0	6	.241
		Joe Haynes	30	27	50	5	8	2	0	0	1	3	8	.160
		Marino Pieretti	27	32	39	5	7	0	0	0	3	4	6	.179
		Randy Gumpert	30	16	29	0	4	0	0	0	1	0	10	.138
		Howie Judson	22	41	29	1	3	1	0	0	2	1	13	.103
		Frank Papish	30	32	27	1	5	2	0	0	4	0	6	.185
		Orval Grove	28	32	21	0	2	0	0	0	0	1	9	.095
		Glen Moulder	30	33	20	3	6	0	1	0	1	1	1	.300
		Bob Gillespie	28	25	16	0	0	0	0	0	1	1	10	.000
		Ike Pearson	31	23	10	0	2	0	0	0	0	0	3	.200
		Earl Caldwell	43	25	5	0	0	0	0	0	1	2	3	.000
		Earl Harrist	28	11	4	0	0	0	0	0	0	0	0	.000
	#	Marv Rotblatt	20	7	4	0	0	0	0	0	0	1	2	.000
	*	Jim Goodwin	21	8	2	0	1	0	0	0	0	0	0	.500
		Fred Bradley	27	8	1	0	0	0	0	0	0	0	0	.000

TEAM PITCHING

Pos		Player	AG	G	ERA	W	L	SV	CG	IP	H	R	ER	BB	HR	SO
SP	*	Bill Wight	26	34	4.80	9	20	1	7	223.3	328	132	119	135	9	68
SP		Joe Haynes	30	27	3.97	9	10	0	6	149.7	167	79	66	52	13	40
SP		Al Gettel	30	22	4.01	8	10	1	7	148.0	154	76	66	60	7	49
SP		Marino Pieretti	27	21	4.95	8	10	1	4	120.0	117	70	66	52	6	28
SP		Randy Gumpert	30	16	3.79	2	6	0	6	97.3	103	43	41	13	6	31
CL		Howie Judson	22	40	4.78	4	5	8	1	107.3	102	60	57	56	7	38
RP		Earl Caldwell	43	25	5.31	1	5	3	0	39.0	53	25	23	22	3	10
RP		Glen Moulder	30	33	6.41	3	6	2	0	85.7	108	67	61	54	8	26

Pos		Player	AG	G	ERA	W	L	SV	CG	IP	H	R	ER	BB	HR	SO
RP		Orval Grove	28	32	6.16	2	10	1	1	87.7	110	64	60	42	6	18
RP		Ike Pearson	31	23	4.92	2	3	1	0	53.0	62	32	29	27	8	12
	*	Frank Papish	30	32	5.00	2	8	4	2	95.3	97	65	53	75	7	41
		Bob Gillespie	28	25	5.12	0	4	0	1	72.0	81	45	41	33	3	19
		Earl Harrist	28	11	5.87	1	3	0	0	23.0	23	17	15	13	4	14
	*	Marv Rotblatt	20	7	7.85	0	1	0	0	18.3	19	16	16	23	0	4
		Fred Bradley	27	8	4.60	0	0	0	0	15.7	11	12	8	4	2	2
	*	Jim Goodwin	21	8	8.71	0	0	1	0	10.3	9	11	10	12	0	3

1949 AMERICAN LEAGUE TEAM STANDINGS

Team	Wins	Losses	WP	GB
New York Yankees	97	57	.630	0
Boston Red Sox	96	58	.623	I
Cleveland Indians	89	65	.578	8
Detroit Tigers	87	67	.565	10
Philadelphia Athletics	81	73	.526	16
Chicago White Sox	63	91	.409	34
St. Louis Browns	53	101	.344	44
Washington Senators	50	104	.325	47

With an inscription reading, *"A great ball player. A great man. A great American,"* the New York Yankees unveiled a monument to the Great Babe Ruth during pre-game ceremonies during their season opener. Also unveiled were plaques honoring Lou Gehrig and Miller Huggins. These monuments still adorn the outfield area at Yankee Stadium known as Monument Park.

1949 is also the year the Yankees signed a young high school player for $1,000. That young ball player was Mickey Mantle. Tom Greenwade, the scout, knew he would never have another moment like that again.

Another Yankee moment in 1949 saw the first six-figure contract with the signing of "Joltin'" Joe DiMaggio for a reported sum of $100,000.

On May 1, 1949, Elmer Valo of the Philadelphia Athletics became the first American Leaguer to slam two bases-loaded triples in a single game. The Athletics went on to win that game over the Washington Senators by a score of 15-9. Valo hit a third bases-loaded triple later in the season to tie the Major League record set by Shano Collins 31 years earlier.

In a show of true fan loyalty, a Cleveland pharmacist named Charley Lupica climbed a flagpole on May 31 and announced he was not coming off his twenty-two foot platform until his beloved Cleveland Indians won another pennant. Poor Charley remained perched atop the flagpole until September 25 with no hope for a pennant for the Indians. He was awarded a brand new car by Cleveland Indians owner, Bill Veeck, for his loyalty.

The 1949 All-Star Game played at Ebbets Field should be noted as the first All-Star Game in which black players made an appearance—a game in which the American League out played the National League by a score of 11-7. Baseball greats such Jackie Robinson, Roy Campanella, Don Newcombe, and Larry Doby all made their All-Star Game debut this year.

The 1940s came to a close with many notable firsts. This was also the only decade in Major League history in which no new ballparks were built. The last ballpark up to that point was Municipal Stadium in Cleveland and the Majors wouldn't see another new ballpark until 1953 with the construction of County Stadium in Milwaukee.

1949 TEAM LEADING HITTING STATISTICS

Statistic	Team	#
Base on Balls	Boston	835
Batting Average	Boston	.282
Doubles	Boston	272
Hits	Boston	1,500
Home Runs	Boston	131
On Base Percentage	Boston	.381
Runs	Boston	896
Slugging Average	Boston	.420
Stolen Bases	Chicago	62
Triples	Chicago	66

1949 TEAM LEADING PITCHING STATISTICS

Statistic	Team	#
Complete Games	Philadelphia	85
ERA	Cleveland	3.36
Fewest Hits Allowed	New York	1,231
Fewest Home Runs Allowed	Washington	79
Fewest Walks Allowed	Cleveland	611
Saves	New York	36
Shutouts	Detroit	19
Strikeouts	New York	671

1949 INDIVIDUAL LEADING HITTING STATISTICS

Statistic	Name(s)	Team	#
Base on Balls	Ted Williams	Boston	162
Batting Average	George Kell	Detroit	.343
Doubles	Ted Williams	Boston	39
Hits	Dale Mitchell	Cleveland	203
Home Runs	Ted Williams	Boston	43
On Base Percentage	Ted Williams	Boston	.490
RBI	Vern Stephens	Boston	159
	Ted Williams	Boston	
Runs	Ted Williams	Boston	150
Slugging Average	Ted Williams	Boston	.650
Stolen Bases	Bob Dillinger	St. Louis	20
Total Bases	Ted Williams	Boston	368
Triples	Dale Mitchell	Cleveland	23

1949 INDIVIDUAL LEADING PITCHING STATISTICS

Statistic	Name(s)	Team	#
Complete Games	Mel Parnell	Boston	27
ERA	Mike Garcia	Cleveland	2.36
Games	Joe Page	New York	60
Saves	Joe Page	New York	27
Shutouts	Ellis Kinder	Boston	6
	Virgil Trucks	Detroit	
Strikeouts	Virgil Trucks	Detroit	153
Winning Percentage	Ellis Kinder	Boston	.793
Wins	Mel Parnell	Boston	25

* * * * *

NEW YORK YANKEES NOTES

Ballpark: Yankee Stadium
Manager: Casey Stengel
Runs Scored: 829
Runs Allowed: 637
Total Attendance: 2,283,676

TEAM BATTING

Pos		Player	AG	G	AB	R	H	2B	3B	HR	RBI	BB	SO	BA
C	*	Yogi Berra	24	116	415	59	115	20	2	20	91	22	25	.277
1B	*	Tommy Henrich	36	115	411	90	118	20	3	24	85	86	34	.287
2B		Jerry Coleman	24	128	447	54	123	21	5	2	42	63	44	.275
3B	*	Bobby Brown	24	104	343	61	97	14	4	6	61	38	18	.283
SS		Phil Rizzuto	31	153	614	110	169	22	7	5	65	72	34	.275
OF	*	Cliff Mapes	27	111	304	56	75	13	3	7	38	58	50	.247

Pos		Player	AG	G	AB	R	H	2B	3B	HR	RBI	BB	SO	BA
OF	*	Gene Woodling	26	112	296	60	80	13	7	5	44	52	21	.272
OF		Hank Bauer	26	103	301	56	82	6	6	10	45	37	42	.272
		Billy Johnson	30	113	329	48	82	11	3	8	56	48	44	.249
		Joe DiMaggio	34	76	272	58	94	14	6	14	67	55	18	.346
		Johnny Lindell	32	78	211	33	51	10	0	6	27	35	27	.242
	*	Dick Kryhoski	24	54	177	18	52	10	3	1	27	9	17	.294
		Snuffy Stirnweiss	30	70	157	29	41	8	2	0	11	29	20	.261
		Charlie Silvera	24	58	130	8	41	2	0	0	13	18	5	.315
	*	Charlie Keller	32	60	116	17	29	4	1	3	16	25	15	.250
		Jack Phillips	27	45	91	16	28	4	1	1	10	12	9	.308
		Gus Niarhos	28	32	43	7	12	2	1	0	6	13	8	.279
	*	Fenton Mole	24	10	27	2	5	2	1	0	2	3	5	.185
	*	Johnny Mize	36	13	23	4	6	1	0	1	2	4	2	.261
	*	Jim Delsing	23	9	20	5	7	1	0	1	3	1	2	.350
	*	Joe Collins	26	7	10	2	1	0	0	0	4	6	2	.100
		Ralph Houk	29	5	7	0	4	0	0	0	1	0	1	.571
		Mickey Witek	33	1	1	0	1	0	0	0	0	0	0	1.00
	*	Tommy Byrne	29	35	83	8	16	4	2	0	13	2	20	.193
		Vic Raschi	30	38	83	7	13	1	1	0	6	13	19	.157
		Allie Reynolds	32	37	78	8	17	3	2	0	10	13	15	.218
	*	Ed Lopat	31	31	76	9	20	8	0	1	4	7	8	.263
	*	Joe Page	31	60	40	2	7	0	0	0	5	1	14	.175
	#	Fred Sanford	29	29	34	1	4	0	0	0	1	1	9	.118
		Bob Porterfield	25	12	19	0	1	1	0	0	0	1	3	.053
		Spec Shea	28	20	12	1	3	0	0	0	4	2	2	.250
		Duane Pillette	26	12	11	0	0	0	0	0	0	2	2	.000
		Cuddles Marshall	24	21	9	0	1	0	0	0	0	1	2	.111
		Ralph Buxton	35	14	13	0	0	0	0	0	0	0	2	.000
		Frank Hiller	28	4	2	0	1	0	0	0	0	0	0	.500
		Hugh Casey	35	4	1	0	0	0	0	0	1	0	0	.000

TEAM PITCHING

Pos		Player	AG	G	ERA	W	L	SV	CG	IP	H	R	ER	BB	HR	SO
SP		Vic Raschi	30	38	3.34	21	10	0	21	274.7	247	120	102	138	16	124
SP		Allie Reynolds	32	35	4.00	17	6	1	4	213.7	200	102	95	123	15	105
SP	*	Tommy Byrne	29	32	3.72	15	7	0	12	196.0	125	84	81	179	11	129
SP	*	Ed Lopat	31	31	3.26	15	10	1	14	215.3	222	93	78	69	19	70
CL	*	Joe Page	31	60	2.59	13	8	27	0	135.3	103	44	39	75	8	99
RP		Cuddles Marshall	24	21	5.11	3	0	3	0	49.3	48	31	28	48	3	13
RP		Fred Sanford	29	29	3.87	7	3	0	3	95.3	100	53	41	57	9	51
RP		Spec Shea	28	20	5.33	1	1	1	0	52.3	48	36	31	43	5	22
RP		Ralph Buxton	35	14	4.05	0	1	2	0	26.7	22	13	12	6	3	14
		Bob Porterfield	25	12	4.06	2	5	0	3	57.7	53	26	26	29	3	25
		Duane Pillette	26	12	4.34	2	4	0	2	37.3	43	20	18	19	6	9
		Hugh Casey	35	4	8.22	1	0	0	0	7.7	11	10	7	8	0	5
		Frank Hiller	28	4	5.87	0	2	1	0	7.7	9	5	5	7	0	3
		Wally Hood	23	2	0.00	0	0	0	0	2.3	0	0	0	1	0	2

* * * * *

BOSTON RED SOX NOTES

Ballpark:	Fenway Park
Manager:	Joe McCarthy
Runs Scored:	896
Runs Allowed:	667
Total Attendance:	1,596,650

TEAM BATTING

Pos		Player	AG	G	AB	R	H	2B	3B	HR	RBI	BB	SO	BA
C		Birdie Tebbetts	36	122	403	42	109	14	0	5	48	62	22	.270
1B	*	Billy Goodman	23	122	443	54	132	23	3	0	56	58	21	.298
2B		Bobby Doerr	31	139	541	91	167	30	9	18	109	75	33	.309

Pos		Player	AG	G	AB	R	H	2B	3B	HR	RBI	BB	SO	BA
3B	*	Johnny Pesky	29	148	604	111	185	27	7	2	69	100	19	.306
SS		Vern Stephens	28	155	610	113	177	31	2	39	159	101	73	.290
OF	*	Ted Williams	30	155	566	150	194	39	3	43	159	162	48	.343
OF		Dom DiMaggio	32	145	605	126	186	34	5	8	60	96	55	.307
OF	*	Al Zarilla	30	124	474	68	133	32	4	9	71	48	51	.281
		Matt Batts	27	60	157	23	38	9	1	3	31	25	22	.242
		Billy Hitchcock	32	55	147	22	30	6	1	0	9	17	11	.204
		Tommy O'Brien	30	49	125	24	28	5	0	3	10	21	12	.224
		Sam Mele	26	18	46	1	9	1	1	0	7	7	14	.196
		Walt Dropo	26	11	41	3	6	2	0	0	1	3	7	.146
		Lou Stringer	32	35	41	10	11	4	0	1	6	5	10	.268
	*	Merl Combs	29	14	24	5	5	1	0	0	1	9	0	.208
	*	Stan Spence	34	7	20	3	3	1	0	0	1	6	1	.150
	*	Tom Wright	25	5	4	1	1	1	0	0	1	1	1	.250
		Babe Martin	29	2	2	0	0	0		0	0	0	0	.000
	*	Mel Parnell	27	39	114	9	29	3	0	0	13	3	10	.254
		Ellis Kinder	34	43	92	11	12	2	0	0	7	6	24	.130
		Joe Dobson	32	33	68	5	10	0	0	0	2	10	22	.147
	*	Chuck Stobbs	19	26	53	8	11	2	0	0	5	3	9	.208
		Jack Kramer	31	21	35	4	9	1	0	0	3	9	13	.257
	*	Mickey McDermott	20	12	33	3	7	3	0	0	6	3	6	.212
		Tex Hughson	33	29	22	1	1	0	0	0	0	0	6	.045
		Walt Masterson	29	18	17	4	2	0	0	0	0	3	7	.118
	*	Mickey Harris	32	7	12	1	1	0	0	0	0	1	3	.083
	*	Earl Johnson	30	19	11	1	0	0	0	0	0	1	7	.000
		Frank Quinn	21	8	6	0	1	0	0	0	0	0	3	.167
	*	Windy McCall	23	5	3	1	2	0	0	0	0	0	0	.667
	*	Dave Ferriss	27	4	1	1	1	1	0	0	1	0	0	1.000

TEAM PITCHING

Pos		Player	AG	G	ERA	W	L	SV	CG	IP	H	R	ER	BB	HR	SO
SP	*	Mel Parnell	27	39	2.77	25	7	2	27	295.3	258	102	91	134	8	122
SP		Ellis Kinder	34	43	3.36	23	6	4	19	252.0	251	103	94	99	21	138
SP		Joe Dobson	32	33	3.85	14	12	2	12	212.7	219	103	91	97	12	87
SP	*	Chuck Stobbs	19	26	4.03	11	6	0	10	152.0	145	72	68	75	10	70
SP		Jack Kramer	31	21	5.16	6	8	1	7	111.7	126	70	64	49	8	24
SP	*	Mickey McDermott	20	12	4.05	5	4	0	6	80.0	63	37	36	52	5	50
RP		Tex Hughson	33	29	5.33	4	2	3	0	77.7	82	49	46	41	5	35
RP	*	Earl Johnson	30	19	7.48	3	6	0	0	49.3	65	45	41	29	1	20
RP		Walt Masterson	29	18	4.25	3	4	4	1	55.0	58	30	26	35	2	19
	*	Mickey Harris	32	7	5.02	2	3	0	2	37.7	53	26	21	20	3	14
		Frank Quinn	21	8	2.86	0	0	0	0	22.0	18	7	7	9	2	4
	*	Windy McCall	23	5	11.57	0	0	0	0	9.3	13	12	12	10	2	8
		Harry Dorish	27	5	2.35	0	0	0	0	7.7	7	2	2	1	1	5
		Dave Ferriss	27	4	4.05	0	0	0	0	6.7	7	3	3	4	1	1
		Jack Robinson	28	3	2.25	0	0	0	0	4.0	4	1	1	1	0	1
		Johnnie Wittig	35	1	9.00	0	0	0	0	2.0	2	2	2	2	0	0
		Denny Galehouse	37	2	13.50	0	0	0	0	2.0	4	3	3	3	1	0

* * * * *

CLEVELAND INDIANS NOTES

Ballpark: Cleveland Stadium
Manager: Lou Boudreau
Runs Scored: 675
Runs Allowed: 574
Total Attendance: 2,233,771

TEAM BATTING

Pos		Player	AG	G	AB	R	H	2B	3B	HR	RBI	BB	SO	BA
C		Jim Hegan	28	152	468	54	105	19	5	8	55	49	89	.224
1B	*	Mickey Vernon	31	153	584	72	170	27	4	18	83	58	51	.291
2B		Joe Gordon	34	148	541	74	136	18	3	20	84	83	33	.251
3B		Ken Keltner	32	80	246	35	57	9	2	8	30	38	26	.232
SS		Lou Boudreau	31	134	475	53	135	20	3	4	60	70	10	.284
OF	*	Dale Mitchell	27	149	640	81	203	16	23	3	56	43	11	.317
OF	*	Larry Doby	25	147	547	106	153	25	3	24	85	91	90	.280
OF		Bob Kennedy	28	121	424	49	117	23	5	9	57	37	40	.276
		Ray Boone	25	86	258	39	65	4	4	4	26	38	17	.252
	*	Thurman Tucker	31	80	197	28	48	5	2	0	14	18	19	.244
		Johnny Beradino	32	50	116	11	23	6	1	0	13	14	14	.198
		Allie Clark	26	35	74	8	13	4	0	1	9	4	7	.176
	*	Luke Easter	33	21	45	6	10	3	0	0	2	8	6	.222
		Al Rosen	25	23	44	3	7	2	0	0	5	7	4	.159
		Mike Tresh	35	38	37	4	8	0	0	0	1	5	7	.216
	*	Hal Peck	32	33	29	1	9	1	0	0	9	3	3	.310
		Minnie Minoso	26	9	16	2	3	0	0	1	1	2	2	.187
	*	Hank Edwards	30	5	15	3	4	0	0	1	1	1	2	.267
		Bobby Avila	25	31	14	3	3	0	0	0	3	1	3	.214
	*	Milt Nielsen	24	3	9	1	1	0	0	0	0	2	4	.111
		Herman Reich	31	1	2	0	1	0	0	0	0	1	0	.500
		Fred Marsh	25	1	0	0	0	0	0	0	0	0	0	.000
	*	Bob Lemon	28	46	108	17	29	6	2	7	19	10	20	.269
		Bob Feller	30	36	72	7	17	2	1	2	10	2	23	.236
	#	Early Wynn	29	35	70	3	10	1	0	1	7	4	10	.143
		Mike Garcia	25	41	51	7	12	2	0	1	7	3	9	.235
	*	Gene Bearden	28	32	45	3	5	0	0	0	1	2	11	.111
		Al Benton	38	40	38	1	5	0	0	0	1	1	11	.132
	#	Steve Gromek	29	27	24	2	4	1	0	0	1	2	5	.167

Pos		Player	AG	G	AB	R	H	2B	3B	HR	RBI	BB	SO	BA
		Satchel Paige	42	31	16	0	1	0	0	0	0	2	4	.062
		Frank Papish	31	25	8	1	1	0	0	0	0	2	1	.125
	*	Sam Zoldak	30	27	8	1	3	0	0	0	0	0	2	.375

TEAM PITCHING

Pos		Player	AG	G	ERA	W	L	SV	CG	IP	H	R	ER	BB	HR	SO
SP		Bob Lemon	28	37	2.99	22	10	1	22	279.7	211	101	93	137	19	138
SP		Bob Feller	30	36	3.75	15	14	0	15	211.0	198	104	88	84	18	108
SP		Early Wynn	29	26	4.15	11	7	0	6	164.7	186	84	76	57	8	62
SP	*	Gene Bearden	28	32	5.10	8	8	0	5	127.0	140	77	72	92	6	41
CL		Al Benton	38	40	2.12	9	6	10	4	135.7	116	33	32	51	7	41
RP	*	Sam Zoldak	30	27	4.25	1	2	0	0	53.0	60	30	25	18	4	11
RP		Satchel Paige	42	31	3.04	4	7	5	1	83.0	70	29	28	33	4	54
RP	*	Frank Papish	31	25	3.19	1	0	1	1	62.0	54	24	22	39	2	23
RP		Mike Garcia	25	41	2.36	14	5	2	8	175.7	154	51	46	60	6	94
		Steve Gromek	29	27	3.33	4	6	0	3	92.0	86	41	34	40	8	22

* * * * *

DETROIT TIGERS NOTES

Ballpark:	Briggs Stadium
Manager:	Red Rolfe
Runs Scored:	751
Runs Allowed:	655
Total Attendance:	1,821,204

TEAM BATTING

Pos		Player	AG	G	AB	R	H	2B	3B	HR	RBI	BB	SO	BA
C	*	Aaron Robinson	34	110	331	38	89	12	0	13	56	73	21	.269
1B	*	Paul Campbell	31	87	255	38	71	15	4	3	30	24	32	.278

Pos		Player	AG	G	AB	R	H	2B	3B	HR	RBI	BB	SO	BA
2B		Neil Berry	27	109	329	38	78	9	1	0	18	27	24	.237
3B		George Kell	26	134	522	97	179	38	9	3	59	71	13	.343
SS		Johnny Lipon	26	127	439	57	110	14	6	3	59	75	24	.251
OF	*	Vic Wertz	24	155	608	96	185	26	6	20	133	80	61	.304
OF		Hoot Evers	28	132	432	68	131	21	6	7	72	70	38	.303
OF		Johnny Groth	22	103	348	60	102	19	5	11	73	65	27	.293
		Don Kolloway	30	126	483	71	142	19	3	2	47	49	25	.294
	*	Pat Mullin	31	104	310	55	83	8	6	12	59	42	29	.268
		Eddie Lake	33	94	240	38	47	9	1	1	15	61	33	.196
		Bob Swift	34	74	189	16	45	6	0	2	18	26	20	.238
	*	George Vico	25	67	142	15	27	5	2	4	18	21	17	.190
	*	Dick Wakefield	28	59	126	17	26	3	1	6	19	32	24	.206
		Hank Riebe	27	17	33	1	6	2	0	0	2	0	5	.182
		Jimmy Outlaw	36	5	4	1	1	0	0	0	0	0	1	.250
		Don Lund	26	2	2	0	0	0	0	0	0	0	1	.000
	*	Bob Mavis	31	1	0	0	0	0	0	0	0	0	0	.000
	*	Earl Rapp	28	1	0	0	0	0	0	0	0	1	0	.000
		Virgil Trucks	32	41	100	6	12	2	0	0	3	1	15	.120
	*	Hal Newhouser	28	38	91	8	18	3	0	0	6	12	19	.198
		Art Houtteman	21	36	78	8	19	2	0	0	7	1	14	.244
	*	Fred Hutchinson	29	38	73	12	18	2	1	0	7	8	5	.247
	#	Ted Gray	24	36	63	5	8	0	0	0	0	6	27	.127
		Lou Kretlow	28	25	26	0	0	0	0	0	1	1	16	.000
		Dizzy Trout	34	33	14	2	2	0	0	1	4	0	2	.143
		Marv Grissom	31	27	9	2	2	0	0	0	0	1	3	.222
	*	Marlin Stuart	30	15	6	2	2	0	0	0	1	1	1	.333
		Stubby Overmire	30	14	3	0	1	0	0	0	0	0	2	.333
		Hal White	30	10	3	0	1	0	0	0	0	0	2	.333

TEAM PITCHING

Pos		Player	AG	G	ERA	W	L	SV	CG	IP	H	R	ER	BB	HR	SO
SP	*	Hal Newhouser	28	38	3.36	18	11	1	22	292.0	277	118	109	111	19	144
SP		Virgil Trucks	32	41	2.81	19	11	4	17	275.0	209	95	86	124	16	153
SP	*	Ted Gray	24	34	3.51	10	10	1	8	195.0	163	83	76	103	11	96
SP		Art Houtteman	21	34	3.71	15	10	0	13	203.7	227	101	84	59	19	85
SP		Fred Hutchinson	29	33	2.96	15	7	1	9	188.7	167	70	62	52	18	54
RP		Dizzy Trout	34	33	4.40	3	6	3	0	59.3	68	35	29	21	2	19
RP		Marv Grissom	31	27	6.41	2	4	0	0	39.3	56	32	28	34	6	17
RP		Lou Kretlow	28	25	6.16	3	2	0	1	76.0	85	58	52	69	5	40
RP	*	Stubby Overmire	30	14	9.87	1	3	0	0	17.3	29	21	19	9	2	3
		Marlin Stuart	30	14	9.10	0	2	0	0	29.7	39	33	30	35	3	14
		Hal White	30	9	0.00	1	0	2	0	12.0	5	0	0	4	0	4
		Saul Rogovin	25	5	14.29	0	1	0	0	5.7	13	9	9	7	1	2

* * * * *

PHILADELPHIA ATHLETICS NOTES

Ballpark:	Shibe Park
Manager:	Connie Mack
Runs Scored:	726
Runs Allowed:	725
Total Attendance:	816,514

TEAM BATTING

Pos		Player	AG	G	AB	R	H	2B	3B	HR	RBI	BB	SO	BA
C		Mike Guerra	36	98	298	41	79	14	1	3	31	37	26	.265
1B	*	Ferris Fain	28	150	525	81	138	21	5	3	78	136	51	.263
2B		Pete Suder	33	118	445	44	119	24	6	10	75	23	35	.267
3B		Hank Majeski	32	114	448	62	124	26	5	9	67	29	23	.277
SS		Eddie Joost	33	144	525	128	138	25	3	23	81	149	80	.263

Pos		Player	AG	G	AB	R	H	2B	3B	HR	RBI	BB	SO	BA
OF		Sam Chapman	33	154	589	89	164	24	4	24	108	80	68	.278
OF	*	Elmer Valo	28	150	547	86	155	27	12	5	85	119	32	.283
OF	*	Wally Moses	38	110	308	49	85	19	3	1	25	51	19	.276
	*	Nellie Fox	21	88	247	42	63	6	2	0	21	32	9	.255
		Don White	30	57	169	12	36	6	0	0	10	14	12	.213
	*	Taffy Wright	37	59	149	14	35	2	5	2	25	16	6	.235
		Joe Astroth	26	55	148	18	36	4	1	0	12	21	13	.243
		Buddy Rosar	34	32	95	7	19	2	0	0	6	16	5	.200
		Tod Davis	24	31	75	7	20	0	1	1	6	9	16	.267
	#	Augie Galan	37	12	26	4	8	2	0	0	0	9	2	.308
	*	Hank Biasatti	27	21	24	6	2	2	0	0	2	8	5	.083
		Bobby Estalella	38	8	20	2	5	0	0	0	3	1	2	.250
		Alex Kellner	24	38	92	7	20	1	0	0	10	7	15	.217
	*	Lou Brissie	25	34	90	7	24	2	1	0	6	1	8	.267
		Joe Coleman	26	33	79	4	14	3	0	1	5	5	29	.177
		Dick Fowler	28	31	77	5	18	2	0	0	11	7	10	.234
		Carl Scheib	22	47	72	9	17	2	0	0	10	8	10	.236
		Bobby Shantz	23	33	37	2	7	0	0	0	2	5	6	.189
		Bubba Harris	23	37	24	0	3	0	0	0	1	0	5	.125
		Phil Marchildon	35	7	6	0	1	0	0	0	0	0	3	.167
		Bill McCahan	28	7	5	0	1	0	0	0	0	0	2	.200
		Jim Wilson	27	2	3	0	0	0	0	0	0	0	1	.000

TEAM PITCHING

Pos		Player	AG	G	ERA	W	L	SV	CG	IP	H	R	ER	BB	HR	SO
SP		Joe Coleman	26	33	3.86	13	14	1	18	240.3	249	119	103	127	12	109
SP	*	Lou Brissie	25	34	4.28	16	11	3	18	229.3	220	113	109	118	20	118
SP		Dick Fowler	28	31	3.75	15	11	1	15	213.7	210	108	89	115	13	43

Pos		Player	AG	G	ERA	W	L	SV	CG	IP	H	R	ER	BB	HR	SO
SP	*	Alex Kellner	24	38	3.75	20	12	1	19	245.0	243	120	102	129	18	94
SP		Carl Scheib	22	38	5.12	9	12	0	11	182.7	191	117	104	118	16	43
RP		Bubba Harris	23	37	5.44	1	1	3	0	84.3	92	57	51	42	12	18
RP	*	Bobby Shantz	23	33	3.40	6	8	2	4	127.0	100	50	48	74	9	58
		Bill McCahan	28	7	2.61	1	1	0	0	20.7	23	9	6	9	0	3
		Phil Marchildon	35	7	11.81	0	3	0	0	16.0	24	23	21	19	3	2
		Jim Wilson	27	2	14.40	0	0	0	0	5.0	7	8	8	5	2	2
		Clem Hausmann	29	1	9.00	0	0	0	0	1.0	0	1	1	2	0	0

* * * * *

CHICAGO WHITE SOX NOTES

Ballpark:	Comiskey Park
Manager:	Jack Onslow
Runs Scored:	648
Runs Allowed:	737
Total Attendance:	937,151

TEAM BATTING

Pos		Player	AG	G	AB	R	H	2B	3B	HR	RBI	BB	SO	BA
C		Don Wheeler	26	67	192	17	46	9	2	1	22	27	19	.240
1B	*	Chuck Cress	27	97	353	45	98	17	6	1	44	39	44	.278
2B		Cass Michaels	23	154	561	73	173	27	9	6	83	101	50	.308
3B	*	Floyd Baker	32	125	388	38	101	15	4	1	40	84	32	.260
SS		Luke Appling	42	142	492	82	148	21	5	5	58	121	24	.301
OF	#	Dave Philley	29	146	598	84	171	20	8	0	44	54	51	.286
OF	*	Catfish Metkovich	28	93	338	50	80	9	4	5	45	41	24	.237
OF	*	Herb Adams	21	56	208	26	61	5	3	0	16	9	16	.293

Pos	Player	AG	G	AB	R	H	2B	3B	HR	RBI	BB	SO	BA
	Steve Souchock	30	84	252	29	59	13	5	7	37	25	38	.234
	Gus Zernial	26	73	198	29	63	17	2	5	38	15	26	.318
	Joe Tipton	27	67	191	20	39	5	3	3	19	27	17	.204
	Eddie Malone	29	55	170	17	46	7	2	1	16	29	19	.271
	Johnny Ostrowski	31	49	158	19	42	9	4	5	31	15	41	.266
*	Gordon Goldsberry	21	39	145	25	36	3	2	1	13	18	9	.248
*	Jerry Scala	24	37	120	17	30	7	1	1	13	17	19	.250
*	Billy Bowers	27	26	78	5	15	2	1	0	6	4	5	.192
	Bobby Rhawn	30	24	73	12	15	4	1	0	5	12	8	.205
	Rocky Krsnich	21	16	55	7	12	3	1	1	9	6	4	.218
*	Earl Rapp	28	19	54	3	14	1	1	0	11	5	6	.259
	Fred Hancock	29	39	52	7	7	2	1	0	9	8	9	.135
	Dick Lane	22	12	42	4	5	0	0	0	4	5	3	.119
*	Bill Higdon	25	11	23	3	7	3	0	0	1	6	3	.304
	George Yankowski	26	12	18	0	3	1	0	0	2	0	2	.167
	Jim Baumer	18	8	10	2	4	1	1	0	2	2	1	400
	Don Kolloway	30	4	4	0	0	0	0	0	0	0	1	.000
	Pat Seerey	26	4	4	1	0	0	0	0	0	3	1	.000
*	Bill Wight	27	35	85	7	14	3	0	0	6	6	27	.165
	Randy Gumpert	31	34	84	7	16	1	0	0	6	3	16	.190
#	Bob Kuzava	26	29	56	1	2	0	0	0	1	3	19	.036
*	Billy Pierce	22	39	51	7	9	0	0	0	2	5	15	.176
	Marino Pieretti	28	48	38	6	9	1	0	0	3	0	7	.237
	Howie Judson	23	26	31	0	2	1	0	0	2	1	11	.065
*	Mickey Haefner	36	14	23	0	6	0	0	0	0	4	7	.261
	Max Surkont	27	44	22	1	1	0	0	0	2	4	12	.045
	Al Gettel	31	19	18	2	3	0	0	0	0	2	2	.167
	Ed Klieman	31	18	8	1	2	0	0	0	0	0	2	.250
*	Clyde Shoun	37	16	5	1	1	0	0	0	1	1	0	.200
*	Bob Cain	24	6	3	0	0	0	0	0	0	0	1	.000

Pos		Player	AG	G	AB	R	H	2B	3B	HR	RBI	BB	SO	BA
		Fred Bradley	28	1	1	0	0	0	0	0	0	0	1	.000
	*	Jack Bruner	24	4	1	0	0	0	0	0	0	0	1	.000
		Bill Evans	30	4	1	0	0	0	0	0	0	0	0	.000

TEAM PITCHING

Pos		Player	AG	G	ERA	W	L	SV	CG	IP	H	R	ER	BB	HR	SO
SP	*	Bill Wight	27	35	3.31	15	13	1	14	245.0	254	106	90	96	9	78
SP		Randy Gumpert	31	34	3.81	13	16	1	18	234.0	223	111	99	83	22	78
SP	*	Billy Pierce	22	32	3.88	7	15	0	8	171.7	145	89	74	112	11	95
SP	*	Bob Kuzava	26	29	4.02	10	6	0	9	156.7	139	76	70	91	6	83
SP	*	Mickey Haefner	36	14	4.37	4	6	1	4	80.3	84	40	39	41	9	17
RP		Max Surkont	27	44	4.78	3	5	4	0	96.0	92	61	51	60	9	38
RP		Marino Pieretti	28	39	5.51	4	6	4	0	116.0	131	77	71	54	10	25
RP		Ed Klieman	31	18	3.00	2	0	3	0	33.0	33	15	11	15	2	9
RP	*	Clyde Shoun	37	16	5.79	1	1	0	0	23.3	37	17	15	13	1	8
		Howie Judson	23	26	4.58	1	14	1	3	108.0	114	65	55	70	13	36
		Al Gettel	31	19	6.43	2	5	1	1	63.0	69	48	45	26	12	22
	*	Bob Cain	24	6	2.45	0	0	1	0	11.0	7	3	3	5	0	5
	*	Jack Bruner	24	4	8.22	1	2	0	0	7.7	10	7	7	8	0	4
		Bill Evans	30	4	7.11	0	1	0	0	6.3	6	6	5	8	0	1
		Ernest Groth	27	3	5.40	0	1	0	0	5.0	2	3	3	3	2	1
		Alex Carrasquel	36	3	14.73	0	0	0	0	3.7	8	6	6	4	1	1
		Fred Bailey	28	1	13.50	0	0	0	0	2.0	4	3	3	3	0	0
		Orval Grove	29	1	54.00	0	0	0	0	.07	4	4	4	1	1	1

* * * * *

ST. LOUIS BROWNS NOTES

Ballpark:	Sportsman's Park
Manager:	Zack Taylor
Runs Scored:	667
Runs Allowed:	913
Total Attendance:	270,936

TEAM BATTING

Pos		Player	AG	G	AB	R	H	2B	3B	HR	RBI	BB	SO	BA
C		Sherm Lollar	24	109	284	28	74	9	1	8	49	32	22	.261
1B	*	Jack Graham	32	137	500	71	119	22	1	24	79	61	62	.238
2B		Jerry Priddy	29	145	544	83	158	26	4	11	63	80	81	.290
3B		Bob Dillinger	30	137	544	68	176	22	13	1	51	51	40	.324
SS		Eddie Pellagrini	31	79	235	26	56	8	1	2	15	14	24	.238
OF	*	Dick Kokos	21	143	501	80	131	28	1	23	77	66	91	.261
OF		Roy Sievers	22	140	471	84	144	28	1	16	91	70	75	.306
OF	*	Stan Spence	34	104	314	46	77	13	3	13	45	52	36	.245
	*	Paul Lehner	28	104	297	25	68	13	0	3	37	16	20	.229
		Les Moss	24	97	278	28	81	11	0	10	39	49	32	.291
		Whitely Platt	28	102	244	29	63	8	2	3	29	24	27	.258
		John Sullivan	28	105	243	29	55	8	3	0	18	38	35	.226
		Andy Anderson	26	71	136	10	17	3	0	1	5	14	21	.125
	*	Al Zarilla	30	15	56	10	14	1	0	1	6	8	2	.250
	*	George Elder	28	41	44	9	11	3	0	0	2	4	11	.250
		Owen Friend	22	2	8	1	3	0	0	0	1	0	0	.375
		Al Naples	21	2	7	0	1	1	0	0	0	0	1	.143
		Ken Wood	24	7	6	0	0	0	0	0	0	1	2	.000
	*	Hank Arft	27	6	5	1	1	1	0	0	2	0	1	.200
	*	Frankie Pack	21	1	1	0	0	0	0	0	0	0	1	.000
		Ned Garver	23	55	75	12	14	4	0	0	2	12	8	.187
	*	Cliff Fannin	25	37	55	4	9	1	0	0	4	2	15	.164

Pos		Player	AG	G	AB	R	H	2B	3B	HR	RBI	BB	SO	BA
		Karl Drews	29	31	46	0	0	0	0	0	0	7	22	.000
	*	Bill Kennedy	28	48	40	3	6	0	0	0	1	3	12	.150
		Al Papai	32	42	38	6	3	0	0	0	1	6	20	.079
		Red Embree	31	40	37	2	6	0	0	0	3	3	10	.162
	*	Joe Ostrowski	32	40	37	3	7	2	0	0	3	11	9	.189
		Dick Starr	28	30	23	3	2	0	0	0	0	4	7	.087
		Tom Ferrick	34	51	21	3	3	1	0	0	3	1	5	.143
		Ribs Raney	26	3	6	0	0	0	0	0	0	0	1	.000
		Ray Shore	28	13	5	0	0	0	0	0	0	0	1	.000
		Ralph Winegarner	39	9	5	2	2	0	0	1	2	1	2	.400
		Bob Malloy	31	5	3	0	0	0	0	0	0	0	2	.000
		Ed Albrecht	20	1	2	0	0	0	0	0	0	1	1	.000
		Bob Savage	27	4	1	0	0	0	0	0	0	0	1	.000

TEAM PITCHING

Pos		Player	AG	G	ERA	W	L	SV	CG	IP	H	R	ER	BB	HR	SO
SP		Ned Garver	23	41	3.98	12	17	3	16	223.7	245	126	99	102	14	70
SP		Cliff Fannin	25	30	6.17	8	14	1	5	143.0	177	106	98	93	15	57
SP		Carl Drews	29	31	6.64	4	12	0	3	139.7	180	113	103	66	11	35
SP		Red Embree	31	35	5.37	3	13	1	4	127.3	146	90	76	89	13	24
CL		Tom Ferrick	34	50	3.88	6	4	6	0	104.3	102	51	45	41	9	34
RP	*	Bill Kennedy	28	48	4.69	4	11	1	2	153.7	172	97	80	73	12	69
RP	*	Joe Ostrowski	32	40	4.79	8	8	2	4	141.0	185	94	75	27	16	34
RP		Al Papai	32	42	5.06	4	11	2	6	142.3	175	103	80	81	8	31
RP		Dick Starr	28	30	4.32	1	7	0	1	83.3	96	46	40	48	6	44
		Ray Shore	28	13	10.80	0	1	0	0	23.3	27	30	28	31	3	13
		Ralph Winegarner	39	9	7.56	0	0	0	0	16.7	24	16	14	2	2	8
		Ribs Raney	26	3	7.71	1	2	0	1	16.3	23	15	14	12	2	5
		Bob Malloy	31	5	2.79	1	1	0	0	9.7	6	3	3	7	0	2

Pos		Player	AG	G	ERA	W	L	SV	CG	IP	H	R	ER	BB	HR	SO
		Bob Savage	27	4	6.43	0	0	0	0	7.0	12	5	5	3	1	1
		Ed Albrecht	20	1	5.40	1	0	0	1	5.0	1	3	3	4	0	1
	*	Irv Medlinger	22	3	27.00	0	0	0	0	4.0	11	13	12	3	1	4
		Jim Bilbrey	25	1	18.00	0	0	0	0	1.0	1	2	2	3	0	0

* * * * *

WASHINGTON SENATORS NOTES

Ballpark:	Griffith Stadium
Manager:	Joe Kuhel
Runs Scored:	584
Runs Allowed:	868
Total Attendance:	770,745

TEAM BATTING

Pos		Player	AG	G	AB	R	H	2B	3B	HR	RBI	BB	SO	BA
C		Al Evans	32	109	321	32	87	12	3	2	42	50	19	.271
1B	*	Eddie Robinson	28	143	527	66	155	27	3	18	78	67	30	.294
2B		Al Kozar	27	105	350	46	94	15	2	4	31	25	23	.269
3B		Eddie Yost	22	124	435	57	110	19	7	9	45	91	41	.253
SS		Sam Dente	27	153	590	48	161	24	4	1	53	31	24	.273
OF		Clyde Vollmer	27	129	443	58	112	17	1	14	59	53	62	.253
OF	*	Bud Stewart	33	118	388	58	110	23	4	8	43	49	33	.284
OF	*	Gil Coan	27	111	358	36	78	7	8	3	25	29	58	.218
	*	Sherry Robertson	30	110	374	59	94	17	3	11	42	42	35	.251
		Sam Mele	26	78	264	21	64	12	2	3	25	17	34	.242
	*	Buddy Lewis	32	95	257	25	63	14	4	3	28	41	12	.245
	*	Jake Early	34	53	138	12	34	4	0	1	11	26	11	.246
		Roberto Ortiz	34	40	129	12	36	3	0	1	11	9	12	.279
		Mark Christman	35	49	112	8	24	2	0	3	18	8	7	.214

Pos	Player	AG	G	AB	R	H	2B	3B	HR	RBI	BB	SO	BA
	John Simmons	24	62	93	12	20	0	0	0	5	11	6	.215
	Ralph Weigel	27	34	60	4	14	2	0	0	4	8	6	.233
*	Hal Keller	21	3	3	1	1	0	0	0	0	0	0	.333
	Herman Reich	31	2	2	0	0	0	0	0	0	0	1	.000
	Jay Difani	25	2	1	0	1	1	0	0	0	0	0	1.000
	Sid Hudson	34	40	67	6	16	2	0	0	10	4	4	.239
	Ray Scarborough	31	34	67	4	13	2	0	0	4	4	15	.194
	Paul Calvert	31	35	51	6	7	0	0	0	1	3	9	.137
*	Mickey Harris	32	23	39	1	8	0	0	0	3	8	7	.205
	Lloyd Hittle	25	36	28	2	4	0	0	0	0	0	7	.143
	Dick Weik	21	28	28	3	5	0	0	0	2	1	8	.179
*	Mickey Haefner	36	20	25	1	5	2	0	0	1	3	3	.200
	Joe Haynes	31	37	25	1	6	0	0	0	4	3	4	.240
	Walt Masterson	29	11	18	1	1	0	0	0	0	2	11	.056
	Dick Welteroth	21	52	17	1	1	1	0	0	0	3	5	.059
	Al Gettel	31	16	8	0	0	0	0	0	1	1	2	.000
	Julio Gonzalez	28	13	5	0	1	0	0	0	0	2	3	.200
*	Forrest Thompson	31	10	5	2	3	1	0	0	0	2	0	.600
	Buzz Dozier	20	2	2	0	0	0	0	0	0	0	1	.000
	Jim Pearce	24	2	2	0	0	0	0	0	0	0	1	.000
	Milo Candini	31	3	1	1	1	0	0	0	0	0	0	1.000
	Ed Klieman	31	2	1	0	1	0	0	0	0	0	0	1.000

TEAM PITCHING

Pos	Player	AG	G	ERA	W	L	SV	CG	IP	H	R	ER	BB	HR	SO
SP		Sid Hudson	34	40	4.22	8	17	1	11	209.0	234	117	98	91	11	54
SP		Ray Scarborough	31	34	4.60	13	11	0	11	199.7	204	115	102	88	10	81
SP		Paul Calvert	31	34	5.43	6	17	1	5	160.7	175	111	97	86	11	52
SP	*	Mickey Harris	32	23	5.16	2	12	0	4	129.0	151	82	74	55	8	54

Pos		Player	AG	G	ERA	W	L	SV	CG	IP	H	R	ER	BB	HR	SO
SP		Dick Weik	21	27	5.38	3	12	1	2	95.3	78	61	57	103	5	58
SP	*	Mickey Haefner	36	19	4.42	5	5	0	4	91.7	85	51	45	53	7	23
RP		Dick Welteroth	21	52	7.36	2	5	2	0	95.3	107	83	78	89	6	37
RP		Joe Haynes	31	37	6.26	2	9	2	0	96.3	106	77	67	55	6	19
RP	*	Lloyd Hittle	25	36	4.21	5	7	0	3	109.0	123	62	51	57	2	32
RP		Al Gettel	31	16	5.45	0	2	1	0	34.7	43	24	21	24	4	7
		Walt Masterson	29	10	3.23	3	2	0	3	53.0	42	22	19	21	4	17
		Julio Gonzalez	28	4.7	0.00	0	0	0	0	34.3	33	20	18	27	3	5
	*	Forrest Thompson	31	9	4.41	1	3	0	1	16.3	22	11	8	9	1	8
		Buzz Dozier	20	2	11.37	0	0	0	0	6.3	12	8	8	6	0	1
		Milo Candini	31	3	4.76	0	0	1	0	5.7	4	3	3	1	0	1
		Jim Pearce	24	2	8.44	0	1	0	0	5.3	9	10	5	5	1	1
		Ed Klieman	31	2	18.00	0	0	0	0	3.0	8	6	6	3	0	1
	*	Dizzy Sutherland	27	1	45.00	0	1	0	0	1.0	2	5	5	6	0	0

1950 AMERICAN LEAGUE TEAM STANDINGS

Team	Wins	Losses	WP	GB
New York Yankees	98	56	.636	0
Detroit Tigers	95	59	.617	3
Boston Red Sox	94	60	.610	4
Cleveland Indians	92	62	.597	6
Washington Senators	67	87	.435	31
Chicago White Sox	60	94	.390	39
St. Louis Browns	58	96	.377	40
Philadelphia Athletics	52	102	.338	46

The 1950s started off with quite a show of power. On June 8, 1950, the Boston Red Sox ran all over the St. Louis Browns and the game ended in a 29-4 rout. The Red Sox set several Major League records in this lopsided victory. They had 32 extra bases on long hits in this game and it also earned them the most extra bases on long hits in 51 games. Red Sox leadoff batter, Clyde Vollmer set an individual Major League record as the only batter to go to the plate eight times in eight innings.

On June 18, 1950, not to be outdone by the Red Sox, the Cleveland Indians scored 14 runs in game two of their doubleheader against the Philadelphia Athletics in the first inning to set a modern Major League record, which also tied the record for most runs scored in a single inning. All of the Cleveland Indians except the pitcher, Mike Garcia, batted twice in the first inning. The Indians won the game with a final score of 21-2.

A real pitcher's duel occurred on June 23, 1950 between the New York Yankees and the Detroit Tigers. The teams hit a combined total of 11 home runs and this game marked the first time that nine different players hit home runs in a single game. The Tigers had a four-run fourth inning off the bats of Dizzy Trout, Gerry Priddy, Vic Wertz, and Hoot Evers. Hoot Evers ended the home run rout with his second homer, an inside-the-park homer, in the bottom of the ninth to win the game 10-9.

1950 also saw President Harry Truman toss out two balls at the Washington Senator's opener. He threw one right-handed and the other one left-handed.

1950 TEAM LEADING HITTING STATISTICS

Statistic	Team	#
Base on Balls	Detroit	722
Batting Average	Boston	.302
Doubles	Boston	287
Hits	Boston	1,665
Home Runs	Cleveland	164
On Base Percentage	Boston	.385
Runs	Boston	1,027
Slugging Average	Boston	.464
Stolen Bases	Philadelphia	42
	Washington	
Triples	New York	70

1950 TEAM LEADING PITCHING STATISTICS

Statistic	Team	#
Complete Games	Detroit	72
ERA	Cleveland	3.76
Fewest Hits Allowed	Cleveland	1,289
Fewest Home Runs Allowed	Washington	99
Fewest Walks Allowed	Detroit	553
Saves	New York	31
Shutouts	New York	12
Strikeouts	New York	712

1950 INDIVIDUAL LEADING HITTING STATISTICS

Statistic	Name(s)	Team	#
Base on Balls	Eddie Yost	Washington	141
Batting Average	Billy Goodman	Boston	.354
Doubles	George Kell	Detroit	56
Hits	George Kell	Detroit	218
Home Runs	Al Rosen	Cleveland	37
On Base Percentage	Larry Doby	Cleveland	.442
RBI	Walt Dropo	Boston	144
	Vern Stephens	Boston	
Runs	Dom DiMaggio	Boston	131
Slugging Average	Joe DiMaggio	New York	.585
Stolen Bases	Dom DiMaggio	Boston	15
Total Bases	Walt Dropo	Boston	326
Triples	Dom DiMaggio	Boston	11
	Bobby Doerr	Boston	
	Hoot Evers	Detroit	

1950 INDIVIDUAL LEADING PITCHING STATISTICS

Statistic	Name(s)	Team	#
Complete Games	Ned Garver	St. Louis	22
	Bob Lemon	Cleveland	
ERA	Early Wynn	Cleveland	3.20
Games	Mickey Harris	Washington	53
Saves	Mickey Harris	Washington	15
Shutouts	Art Houtteman	Detroit	4
Strikeouts	Bob Lemon	Cleveland	170

Statistic	Name(s)	Team	#
Winning Percentage	Vic Raschi	New York	.724
Wins	Bob Lemon	Cleveland	23

* * * * *

NEW YORK YANKEES NOTES

Ballpark: Yankee Stadium
Manager: Casey Stengel
Runs Scored: 914
Runs Allowed: 691
Total Attendance: 2,081,380

TEAM BATTING

Pos		Player	AG	G	AB	R	H	2B	3B	HR	RBI	BB	SO	BA
C	*	Yogi Berra	25	151	597	116	192	30	6	28	124	55	12	.322
1B	*	Joe Collins	27	108	205	47	48	8	3	8	28	31	34	.234
2B		Jerry Coleman	25	153	522	69	150	19	6	6	69	67	38	.287
3B		Billy Johnson	31	108	327	44	85	16	2	6	40	42	30	.260
SS		Phil Rizzuto	32	155	617	125	200	36	7	7	66	92	39	.324
OF		Joe DiMaggio	35	139	525	114	158	33	10	32	122	80	33	.301
OF	*	Gene Woodling	27	122	449	81	127	20	10	6	60	70	31	.283
OF		Hank Bauer	27	113	415	72	133	16	2	13	70	35	41	.320
	*	Cliff Mapes	28	108	356	60	88	14	6	12	61	47	61	.247
	*	Bobby Brown	25	95	277	33	74	4	2	4	37	39	18	.267
	*	Johnny Mize	37	90	274	43	76	12	0	25	72	29	24	.277
	*	Tommy Henrich	37	73	151	20	41	6	8	6	34	27	6	.272
		Jackie Jensen	23	45	70	13	12	2	2	1	5	7	8	.171
		Billy Martin	22	43	36	10	9	1	0	1	8	3	3	.250
	*	Johnny Hopp	33	19	27	9	9	2	1	1	8	8	1	.333
		Charlie Silvera	25	18	25	2	4	0	0	0	1	1	2	.160

Pos		Player	AG	G	AB	R	H	2B	3B	HR	RBI	BB	SO	BA
		Johnny Lindell	33	7	21	2	4	0	0	0	2	4	2	.190
	*	Jim Delsing	24	12	10	2	4	0	0	0	2	2	0	.400
		Ralph Houk	30	10	9	0	1	1	0	0	1	0	2	.111
	*	Hank Workman	24	2	5	1	1	0	0	0	0	0	1	.200
		Snuffy Stirnweiss	31	7	2	0	0	0	0	0	0	0	0	.000
	*	Dick Wakefield	29	3	2	0	1	0	0	0	1	1	1	.500
		Gus Niarhos	29	1	0	0	0	0	0	0	0	0	0	.000
		Vic Raschi	31	33	86	6	17	2	0	1	8	7	14	.198
	*	Ed Lopat	32	36	82	14	19	2	3	0	7	17	9	.232
	*	Tommy Bryne	30	34	81	14	22	3	1	2	16	4	15	.272
		Allie Reynolds	33	36	81	5	15	3	1	0	9	7	16	.185
	*	Whitey Ford	21	20	36	2	7	0	0	0	3	4	4	.194
	#	Fred Sanford	30	26	35	4	8	2	0	0	3	1	6	.229
		Tom Ferrick	35	30	14	2	2	1	0	0	0	2	2	.143
	*	Joe Ostrowski	33	21	9	2	1	0	0	0	1	2	1	.111
	*	Joe Page	32	37	8	1	2	1	0	0	2	2	3	.250
		Don Johnson	23	8	3	0	0	0	0	0	0	0	1	.000
		Bob Porterfield	26	11	3	0	1	0	0	0	0	0	0	.333
		Ernie Nevel	31	3	1	0	0	0	0	0	0	0	0	.000
		Dave Madison	29	1	0	1	0	0	0	0	0	1	0	.000

TEAM PITCHING

Pos		Player	AG	G	ERA	W	L	SV	CG	IP	H	R	ER	BB	HR	SO
SP	*	Ed Lopat	32	35	3.47	18	8	1	15	236.3	244	110	91	65	19	72
SP		Vic Raschi	31	33	4.00	21	8	1	17	256.7	232	120	114	116	19	155
SP	*	Tommy Byrne	30	31	4.74	15	9	0	10	203.3	188	115	107	160	23	118
SP		Allie Reynolds	33	35	3.74	16	12	2	14	240.7	215	108	100	138	12	160
SP	*	Whitey Ford	21	20	2.81	9	1	1	7	112.0	87	39	35	52	7	59

Pos		Player	AG	G	ERA	W	L	SV	CG	IP	H	R	ER	BB	HR	SO
CL	*	Joe Page	32	37	5.04	3	7	13	0	55.3	66	34	31	31	8	33
RP		Tom Ferrick	35	30	3.65	8	4	9	0	56.7	49	26	23	22	5	20
RP	*	Joe Ostrowski	33	21	5.15	1	1	3	1	43.7	50	26	25	15	11	15
RP		Fred Sanford	30	26	4.55	5	4	0	2	112.7	103	60	57	79	9	54
		Bob Porterfield	26	10	8.69	1	1	1	0	19.7	28	19	19	8	2	9
		Don Johnson	23	8	10.00	1	0	0	0	18.0	35	21	20	12	2	9
		Duane Pillette	27	4	1.29	0	0	0	0	7.0	9	3	1	3	0	4
		Ernie Nevel	31	3	9.95	0	1	0	0	6.3	10	7	7	5	0	3
		Dave Madison	29	1	6.00	0	0	0	0	3.0	3	2	2	1	1	1
		Lew Burdette	23	2	6.75	0	0	0	0	1.3	3	1	1	0	0	0

* * * * *

DETROIT TIGERS NOTES

Ballpark: Briggs Stadium
Manager: Red Rolfe
Runs Scored: 837
Runs Allowed: 713
Total Attendance: 1,951,474

TEAM BATTING

Pos		Player	AG	G	AB	R	H	2B	3B	HR	RBI	BB	SO	BA
C	*	Aaron Robinson	35	107	283	37	64	7	0	9	37	75	35	.226
1B		Don Kolloway	31	125	467	55	135	20	4	6	62	29	28	.289
2B		Jerry Priddy	30	157	618	104	171	26	6	13	75	95	95	.277
3B		George Kell	27	157	641	114	218	56	6	8	101	66	18	.340
SS		Johnny Lipon	27	147	601	104	176	27	6	2	63	81	26	.293
OF		Johnny Groth	23	157	566	95	173	30	8	12	85	95	27	.306
OF	*	Vic Wertz	25	149	559	99	172	37	4	27	123	91	55	.308
OF		Hoot Evers	29	143	526	100	170	35	11	21	103	71	40	.323

Pos		Player	AG	G	AB	R	H	2B	3B	HR	RBI	BB	SO	BA
	*	Dick Kryhoski	25	53	169	20	37	10	9	4	18	8	11	.219
	*	Pat Mullin	32	69	142	16	31	5	0	6	23	20	23	.218
		Bob Swift	35	67	132	14	30	4	0	2	9	25	6	.227
	*	Joe Ginsberg	23	36	95	12	22	6	0	0	12	11	6	.232
	*	Charlie Keller	33	50	51	7	16	1	3	2	16	13	6	.314
		Neil Berry	28	39	40	9	10	1	0	0	7	6	11	.250
		Eddie Lake	34	20	7	3	0	0	0	0	1	1	3	.000
	*	Frank House	20	5	5	1	2	1	0	0	0	0	1	.400
	*	Paul Campbell	32	3	1	1	0	0	0	0	0	0	0	.000
	*	Fred Hutchinson	30	44	95	15	31	7	0	0	20	12	3	.326
		Art Houtteman	22	41	93	5	14	4	1	0	3	5	20	.151
	*	Hal Newhouser	29	35	74	6	13	2	0	0	8	5	8	.176
		Dizzy Trout	35	34	63	6	12	1	1	1	10	6	20	.190
#		Ted Gray	25	27	50	4	7	2	0	0	3	4	22	.140
		Hal White	31	42	33	1	4	2	0	0	1	0	10	.121
		Virgil Trucks	33	7	20	2	3	1	0	0	0	0	2	.150
		Saul Rogovin	26	11	16	2	3	0	0	1	5	0	3	.187
	*	Marlin Stuart	31	19	12	2	1	0	0	0	0	1	1	.083
		Hank Borowy	34	13	7	1	1	0	0	0	1	0	1	.143
		Paul Calvert	32	32	7	2	0	0	0	0	1	1	0	.000
		Ray Herbert	20	8	7	0	2	0	0	0	0	0	0	.286
	*	Bill Connelly	25	2	1	0	0	0	0	0	0	1	0	.000

TEAM PITCHING

Pos		Player	AG	G	ERA	W	L	SV	CG	IP	H	R	ER	BB	HR	SO
SP		Art Houtteman	22	41	3.54	19	12	4	21	274.7	257	112	108	99	29	88
SP	*	Hal Newhouser	29	35	4.34	15	13	3	15	213.7	232	110	103	81	23	87
SP		Fred Hutchinson	30	39	3.96	17	8	0	10	231.7	269	119	102	48	18	71
SP	*	Ted Gray	25	27	4.40	10	7	1	7	149.3	139	85	73	72	22	102
SP		Dizzy Trout	35	34	3.75	13	5	4	11	184.7	190	84	77	64	13	88

Pos	Player	AG	G	ERA	W	L	SV	CG	IP	H	R	ER	BB	HR	SO
RP	Hal White	31	42	4.54	9	6	1	3	111.0	96	59	56	65	7	53
RP	Paul Calvert	32	32	6.31	2	2	4	0	51.3	71	42	36	25	7	14
RP	Marlin Stuart	31	19	5.56	3	1	2	0	43.7	59	32	27	22	6	19
RP	Hank Borowy	34	13	3.31	1	1	0	1	32.7	23	15	12	16	3	12
	Virgil Trucks	33	7	3.54	3	1	0	2	48.3	45	20	19	21	6	25
	Saul Rogovin	26	11	4.50	2	1	0	1	40.0	39	21	20	26	5	11
	Ray Herbert	20	8	3.63	1	2	1	1	22.3	20	11	9	12	1	5
	Bill Connelly	25	2	6.75	0	0	0	0	4.0	4	3	3	2	1	1

* * * * *

BOSTON RED SOX NOTES

Ballpark: Fenway Park
Manager: Joe McCarthy and Steve O'Neill
Runs Scored: 1027
Runs Allowed: 804
Total Attendance: 1,344,080

TEAM BATTING

Pos		Player	AG	G	AB	R	H	2B	3B	HR	RBI	BB	SO	BA
C		Birdie Tebbetts	37	79	268	33	83	10	1	8	45	29	26	.310
1B		Walt Dropo	27	136	559	101	180	28	8	34	144	45	75	.322
2B		Bobby Doerr	32	149	586	103	172	29	11	27	120	67	42	.294
3B	*	Johnny Pesky	30	127	490	112	153	22	6	1	49	104	31	.312
SS		Vern Stephens	29	149	628	125	185	34	6	30	144	65	43	.295
OF		Dom DiMaggio	33	141	588	131	193	30	11	7	70	82	68	.328
OF	*	Al Zarilla	31	130	471	92	153	32	10	9	74	76	47	.325
OF	*	Ted Williams	31	89	334	82	106	24	1	28	97	82	21	.317
	*	Billy Goodman	24	110	424	91	150	25	3	4	68	52	25	.354
		Matt Batts	28	75	238	27	65	15	3	4	34	18	19	.273

Pos	Player	AG	G	AB	R	H	2B	3B	HR	RBI	BB	SO	BA
	Clyde Vollmer	28	57	169	35	48	10	0	7	37	21	35	.284
*	Tom Wright	26	54	107	17	34	7	0	0	20	6	18	.318
	Buddy Rosar	35	27	84	13	25	2	0	1	12	7	4	.298
	Tommy O'Brien	31	9	31	0	4	1	0	0	3	3	5	.129
	Ken Keltner	33	13	28	2	9	2	0	0	2	3	6	.321
	Lou Stringer	33	24	17	7	5	1	0	0	2	0	4	.294
*	Fred Hatfield	25	10	12	3	3	0	0	0	2	3	1	.250
*	Charlie Maxwell	23	3	8	1	0	0	0	0	0	1	3	.000
*	Jim Piersall	20	6	7	4	2	0	0	0	0	4	0	.286
*	Merle Combs	30	1	0	0	0	0	0	0	0	1	0	.000
	Bob Scherbarth	24	1	0	0	0	0	0	0	0	0	0	.000
*	Mel Parnell	28	40	98	7	19	5	0	0	7	5	13	.194
	Ellis Kinder	35	48	71	5	13	1	1	1	11	2	13	.183
	Joe Dobson	33	39	70	6	1	2	0	0	9	9	23	.214
*	Chuck Stobbs	20	32	57	8	14	1	0	0	9	12	16	.246
	Walt Masterson	30	33	44	2	6	1	0	0	1	2	18	.136
*	Mickey McDermott	21	39	44	11	16	5	0	0	12	9	3	.364
*	Willard Nixon	22	22	36	3	5	0	0	0	2	5	7	.139
	Al Papai	33	16	17	3	3	0	0	0	0	3	3	.176
	Charlie Schanz	31	14	11	2	1	0	0	0	0	1	5	.091
	Harry Taylor	31	3	7	1	2	0	0	0	0	0	0	.286
*	Dick Littlefield	24	15	4	0	0	0	0	0	0	0	3	.000
	Jim McDonald	23	9	3	0	1	0	0	0	0	2	1	.333
*	James Atkins	29	1	2	0	0	0	0	0	0	0	2	.000
*	Earl Johnson	31	11	2	0	0	0	0	0	0	0	0	.000
	Gordie Mueller	27	8	1	0	0	0	0	0	0	0	0	.000

TEAM PITCHING

Pos		Player	AG	G	ERA	W	L	SV	CG	IP	H	R	ER	BB	HR	SO
SP	*	Mel Parnell	29	40	3.61	18	10	3	21	249.0	244	116	100	106	17	93
SP		Joe Dobson	33	39	4.18	15	10	4	12	206.7	217	103	96	81	15	81
SP	*	Chuck Stobbs	20	32	5.10	12	7	1	6	169.3	158	104	96	88	17	78
SP		Willard Nixon	22	22	6.04	8	6	2	2	101.3	126	75	68	58	8	57
CL		Ellis Kinder	35	48	4.26	14	12	9	11	207.0	212	105	98	78	23	95
RP	*	Mickey McDermott	21	38	5.19	7	3	5	4	130.0	119	80	75	124	8	96
RP		Walt Masterson	30	33	5.64	8	6	1	6	129.3	145	91	81	82	15	60
RP		Charley Schanz	31	14	8.34	3	2	0	0	22.7	25	21	21	24	3	14
RP	*	Dick Littlefield	24	15	9.26	2	2	1	0	23.3	27	25	24	24	6	13
		Al Papai	33	16	6.75	4	2	2	2	50.7	61	41	38	28	5	19
		Harry Taylor	31	3	1.42	2	0	0	2	19.0	13	3	3	8	0	8
		Jim McDonald	23	9	3.79	1	0	0	0	19.0	23	9	8	10	1	5
	*	Earl Johnson	31	11	7.24	0	0	0	0	13.7	18	11	11	8	0	6
		Gordie Mueller	27	8	10.29	0	0	0	0	7.0	11	8	8	13	1	1
		James Atkins	29	1	3.86	0	0	0	0	4.7	4	2	2	4	1	0
		Jim Suchecki	23	4	4.50	0	0	0	0	4.0	3	2	2	4	0	3
		Frank Quinn	22	1	9.00	0	0	0	0	2.0	2	2	2	1	0	0
		Bob Gillespie	30	1	20.25	0	0	0	0	1.3	2	3	3	4	1	0
		Phil Marchildon	36	1	6.75	0	0	0	0	1.3	1	1	1	2	0	0
		Dave Ferriss	28	1	18.00	0	0	0	0	1.0	2	2	2	1	0	1

* * * * *

CLEVELAND INDIANS NOTES

Ballpark:	Cleveland Stadium
Manager:	Lou Boudreau
Runs Scored:	806
Runs Allowed:	654
Total Attendance:	1,727,464

TEAM BATTING

Pos		Player	AG	G	AB	R	H	2B	3B	HR	RBI	BB	SO	BA
C		Jim Hegan	29	131	415	53	91	16	5	14	58	42	52	.219
1B	*	Luke Easter	34	141	540	96	151	20	4	28	107	70	95	.280
2B		Joe Gordon	35	119	368	59	87	12	1	19	57	56	44	.236
3B		Al Rosen	26	155	554	100	159	23	4	37	116	100	72	.287
SS		Ray Boone	26	109	365	53	110	14	6	7	58	56	27	.301
OF		Bob Kennedy	29	146	540	79	157	27	5	9	54	53	31	.291
OF	*	Larry Doby	26	142	503	110	164	25	5	25	102	98	71	.326
OF	*	Dale Mitchell	28	130	506	81	156	27	5	3	49	67	21	.308
		Lou Boudreau	32	81	260	23	70	13	2	1	29	31	5	.269
		Bobby Avila	26	80	201	39	60	10	2	1	21	29	17	.299
		Allie Clark	27	59	163	19	35	6	1	6	21	11	10	.215
		Ray Murray	32	55	139	16	38	8	2	1	13	12	13	.273
	*	Thurman Tucker	32	57	101	13	18	2	0	1	7	14	17	.178
	*	Mickey Vernon	32	28	90	8	17	0	0	0	10	12	10	.189
		Jim Lemon	22	12	34	4	6	1	0	1	1	3	12	.176
	*	Herb Conyers	29	7	9	2	3	0	0	1	1	1	2	.333
		Johnny Beradino	33	4	5	1	2	0	0	0	3	1	0	.400
	*	Bob Lemon	29	72	136	21	37	9	1	6	26	13	25	.272
		Bob Feller	31	35	83	7	10	0	1	2	5	5	33	.120
	#	Early Wynn	30	39	77	12	18	5	1	2	10	10	12	.322
		Mike Garcia	26	33	65	4	13	2	0	0	6	1	25	.200
	#	Steve Gromek	30	31	38	1	6	0	0	0	1	1	9	.158
	*	Sam Zoldak	31	33	16	2	3	0	0	0	2	2	0	.187
	*	Gene Bearden	29	14	13	2	2	1	1	0	0	2	2	.154
		Al Benton	39	36	12	1	1	0	0	0	0	2	9	.083
		Jesse Flores	35	28	11	0	0	0	0	0	0	0	2	.000
		Marino Pieretti	29	30	7	0	2	0	0	0	1	0	2	.286
	*	Dick Rozek	23	12	5	0	0	0	0	0	0	0	3	.000

Pos		Player	AG	G	AB	R	H	2B	3B	HR	RBI	BB	SO	BA
		Dick Weik	22	11	5	0	1	1	0	0	0	0	4	.200
	*	Al Aber	22	1	2	0	0	0	0	0	0	1	1	.000

TEAM PITCHING

Pos		Player	AG	G	ERA	W	L	SV	CG	IP	H	R	ER	BB	HR	SO
SP		Bob Lemon	29	44	3.84	23	11	3	22	288.0	281	144	123	146	28	170
SP		Bob Feller	31	35	3.43	16	11	0	16	247.0	230	105	94	103	20	119
SP		Mike Garcia	26	33	3.86	11	11	0	11	184.0	191	88	79	74	15	76
SP		Early Wynn	30	32	3.20	18	8	0	14	213.7	166	88	76	101	20	143
RP		Al Benton	39	36	3.57	4	2	4	0	63.0	57	32	25	30	7	26
RP	*	Sam Zoldak	31	33	3.96	4	2	4	0	63.7	64	33	28	21	6	15
RP		Marino Pieretti	29	29	4.18	0	1	1	0	47.3	45	24	22	30	2	11
RP		Jesse Flores	35	28	3.74	3	3	4	1	53.0	53	24	22	25	3	37
		Steve Gromek	30	31	3.65	10	7	0	4	113.3	94	50	46	36	10	43
	*	Gene Bearden	29	14	6.15	1	3	0	0	45.3	57	32	31	32	5	10
		Dick Weik	22	11	3.81	1	3	0	0	26.0	18	17	11	26	1	16
	*	Dick Rozek	23	12	4.97	0	0	0	0	25.3	28	15	14	19	3	14
	*	Al Aber	22	1	2.00	1	0	0	1	9.0	5	2	2	4	0	4

* * * * *

WASHINGTON SENATORS NOTES

Ballpark:	Griffith Stadium
Manager:	Bucky Harris
Runs Scored:	690
Runs Allowed:	813
Total Attendance:	699,697

TEAM BATTING

Pos		Player	AG	G	AB	R	H	2B	3B	HR	RBI	BB	SO	BA
C		Al Evans	33	90	289	24	68	8	3	2	30	29	21	.235
1B	*	Mickey Vernon	32	90	327	47	100	17	3	9	65	50	29	.306
2B		Cass Michaels	24	106	388	48	97	8	4	4	47	55	39	.250
3B		Eddie Yost	23	155	573	114	169	26	2	11	58	141	63	.295
SS		Sam Dente	28	155	603	56	144	20	5	2	59	39	19	.239
OF	*	Irv Noren	25	138	542	80	160	27	10	14	98	67	77	.295
OF	*	Bud Stewart	34	118	378	46	101	15	6	4	35	46	33	.267
OF		Sam Mele	27	126	435	57	119	21	6	12	86	51	40	.274
	*	Gil Coan	28	104	366	58	111	17	4	7	50	28	46	.303
		Mickey Grasso	30	75	195	25	56	4	1	1	22	25	31	.287
		Johnny Ostrowski	32	55	141	16	32	2	1	4	23	20	31	.227
	*	Eddie Robinson	29	36	129	21	30	4	2	1	13	25	4	.233
	*	Sherry Robertson	31	71	123	19	32	3	3	2	16	22	18	.260
	*	Merl Combs	30	37	102	19	25	1	0	0	6	22	16	.245
		Roberto Ortiz	35	39	75	4	17	2	1	0	8	7	12	.227
		Al Kozar	28	20	55	7	11	1	0	0	3	5	8	.200
	*	Hal Keller	22	11	28	1	6	3	0	1	5	2	2	.214
		Len Okrie	26	17	27	1	6	0	0	0	2	6	7	.222
	*	Fred Taylor	25	6	16	1	2	0	0	0	0	1	2	.125
		Clyde Vollmer	28	6	14	4	4	0	0	0	1	2	3	.286
		Tommy O'Brien	31	3	9	1	1	0	0	0	1	1	0	.111
	*	George Genovese	28	3	1	1	0	0	0	0	0	1	0	.000
		Sid Hudson	35	31	93	10	20	1	1	0	12	1	7	.215
	#	Bob Kuzava	27	22	50	5	5	0	0	1	4	5	23	.100
		Connie Marrero	39	27	49	4	6	1	0	0	3	7	12	.122
		Sandy Consuegra	29	24	40	6	7	1	0	0	4	2	11	.175
		Joe Haynes	32	27	35	3	7	4	1	0	1	1	5	.200
		Al Sima	28	17	26	1	3	0	0	0	0	0	15	.115
	*	Gene Bearden	29	14	22	1	5	1	0	0	0	3	2	.227

Pos		Player	AG	G	AB	R	H	2B	3B	HR	RBI	BB	SO	BA
	*	Steve Nagy	31	15	22	5	5	1	0	1	3	3	5	.227
		Ray Scarborough	32	8	20	2	2	1	0	0	0	1	4	.100
	*	Mickey Harris	33	53	17	2	4	0	0	0	3	3	5	.235
		Lloyd Hittle	26	11	13	0	1	0	0	0	1	1	3	.077
		Jim Pearce	25	20	13	0	2	0	0	0	0	0	5	.154
		Dick Weik	22	14	13	0	2	0	0	0	0	0	3	.154
		Julio Moreno	29	4	8	0	1	0	0	0	0	0	1	.125
		Elmer Singleton	32	21	7	1	3	1	0	0	0	0	3	.429
		Carlos Pascual	19	2	4	0	1	0	0	0	0	0	0	.250
		Bob Ross	21	6	3	0	0	0	0	0	0	0	0	.000

TEAM PITCHING

Pos		Player	AG	G	ERA	W	L	SV	CG	IP	H	R	ER	BB	HR	SO
SP		Sid Hudson	35	30	4.09	14	14	0	17	237.7	261	129	108	98	17	75
SP	*	Bob Kuzava	27	22	3.95	8	7	0	8	155	156	80	68	75	8	84
SP		Connie Marrero	39	27	4.50	6	10	1	8	152	159	84	76	55	17	63
SP		Sandy Consuegra	29	21	4.40	7	8	2	8	124.7	132	71	61	57	6	38
CL	*	Mickey Harris	33	53	4.78	5	9	15	0	98	93	56	52	46	10	41
RP		Elmer Singleton	32	21	5.20	1	2	0	0	36.3	39	23	21	17	4	19
RP		Joe Haynes	32	27	5.84	7	5	0	1	101.7	124	73	66	46	14	15
RP		Jim Pearce	25	20	6.04	2	1	0	1	56.7	48	40	38	37	2	18
	*	Al Sima	28	17	4.79	4	5	0	1	77	89	49	41	26	9	23
	*	Gene Bearden	29	12	4.21	3	5	0	4	68.3	81	35	32	33	1	20
		Ray Scarborough	32	8	4.01	3	5	0	4	58.3	62	30	26	22	1	24
	*	Steve Nagy	31	9	6.58	2	5	0	2	53.3	69	50	39	29	5	17
		Dick Weik	22	14	4.30	1	3	0	1	44.0	38	27	21	47	2	26
	*	Lloyd Hittle	26	11	4.98	2	4	0	1	43.3	60	27	24	17	1	9
		Julio Moreno	29	4	4.64	1	1	0	1	21.3	22	13	11	12	1	7
		Carlos Pascual	19	3	2.12	1	1	0	2	17	12	5	4	8	0	3

Pos		Player	AG	G	ERA	W	L	SV	CG	IP	H	R	ER	BB	HR	SO
	*	Bob Ross	21	6	8.53	0	1	0	0	12.7	15	12	12	15	1	2
		Dick Welteroth	22	5	3.00	0	0	0	0	6	5	5	2	6	0	2
		Rogelio Martinez	31	2	27.00	0	1	0	0	1.3	4	4	4	2	0	0

CHICAGO WHITE SOX NOTES

Ballpark:	Comiskey Park
Manager:	Jack Onslow and Red Corriden
Runs Scored:	625
Runs Allowed:	749
Total Attendance:	781,330

TEAM BATTING

Pos		Player	AG	G	AB	R	H	2B	3B	HR	RBI	BB	SO	BA
C		Phil Masi	34	122	377	38	105	17	2	7	55	49	36	.279
1B	*	Eddie Robinson	29	119	424	62	133	11	2	20	73	60	28	.314
2B	*	Nellie Fox	22	130	457	45	113	12	7	0	30	35	17	.247
3B		Hank Majeski	33	122	414	47	128	18	2	6	46	42	34	.309
SS		Chico Carrasquel	22	141	524	72	148	21	5	4	46	66	46	.282
OF	#	Dave Philley	30	156	619	69	150	21	5	14	80	52	57	.242
OF		Gus Zernial	27	143	543	75	152	16	4	29	93	38	110	.280
OF	*	Marv Rickert	29	64	278	38	66	9	2	4	27	21	42	.237
	*	Floyd Baker	33	83	186	26	59	7	0	0	11	32	10	.317
		Mike McCormick	33	55	138	16	32	4	3	0	10	16	6	.232
		Cass Michaels	24	36	138	21	43	6	3	4	19	13	8	.312
		Luke Appling	43	50	128	11	30	3	4	0	13	12	8	.234
	*	Gordon Goldsberry	22	82	127	19	34	8	2	2	25	26	18	.268
	*	Herb Adams	22	34	118	12	24	2	3	0	2	12	7	.203
		Gus Niarhos	29	41	105	17	34	4	0	0	16	14	6	.324
		Eddie Malone	30	31	71	2	16	2	0	0	10	10	8	.225
	*	Jerry Scala	25	40	67	8	13	2	1	0	6	10	10	.194

Pos		Player	AG	G	AB	R	H	2B	3B	HR	RBI	BB	SO	BA
		Jim Busby	23	18	48	5	10	0	0	0	4	1	5	.208
		Johnny Ostrowski	32	21	45	9	10	1	1	2	2	9	8	.222
		Joe Erautt	28	16	18	0	4	0	0	0	1	1	3	.222
		Al Kozar	28	10	10	4	3	0	0	1	2	0	3	.300
	*	Chuck Kress	28	3	8	0	0	0	0	0	0	0	2	.000
		Ed McGhee	25	3	6	0	1	0	1	0	0	0	1	.167
		Bill Wilson	21	3	6	0	0	0	0	0	0	2	2	.000
		Joe Kirrene	18	1	4	0	1	0	0	0	0	0	1	.250
		Johnny Ostrowski	32	1	4	1	2	1	0	0	0	0	1	.500
	*	Bill Salkeld	33	1	3	0	0	0	0	0	0	1	0	.000
	*	Billy Pierce	23	40	77	10	20	3	0	0	6	6	13	.260
	*	Bob Cain	25	35	61	7	12	2	0	0	2	3	15	.197
	*	Bill Wight	28	30	61	2	0	0	0	0	2	4	17	.000
		Ray Scaarborough	32	27	46	1	8	0	0	0	4	3	7	.174
		Randy Gumpert	32	41	42	2	3	0	0	0	4	2	10	.071
		Ken Holcombe	31	24	32	2	5	1	0	0	0	0	8	.156
	*	Mickey Haefner	37	24	20	0	4	0	0	0	1	3	3	.200
		Howie Judson	24	46	20	1	2	1	0	0	0	3	5	.100
		Luis Aloma	26	42	15	0	1	0	0	0	1	0	6	.067
#		Bob Kuzava	27	10	12	3	1	0	0	0	1	3	3	.083
		Lou Kretlow	29	11	4	0	0	0	0	0	0	0	1	.000
#		Marv Rotblatt	22	2	2	0	0	0	0	0	0	0	1	.000
		Gus Keriazakos	18	1	1	0	1	0	0	0	0	0	0	1.000
		John Perkovich	26	1	1	0	0	0	0	0	0	0	1	.000

TEAM PITCHING

Pos		Player	AG	G	ERA	W	L	SV	CG	IP	H	R	ER	BB	HR	SO
SP	*	Billy Pierce	23	33	3.98	12	16	1	15	219.3	189	112	97	137	11	118
SP	*	Bill Wight	28	30	3.58	10	16	0	13	206.0	213	89	82	79	10	62
SP	*	Bob Cain	25	34	3.93	9	12	2	11	171.7	153	80	75	109	12	77

Pos		Player	AG	G	ERA	W	L	SV	CG	IP	H	R	ER	BB	HR	SO
SP		Ray Scarborough	32	27	5.30	10	13	1	8	149.3	160	95	88	62	10	70
SP		Ken Holcombe	31	24	4.59	5	10	1	5	96.0	122	68	49	45	10	37
RP		Howie Judson	24	46	3.94	2	3	0	1	112.0	105	53	49	63	10	34
RP		Luis Aloma	26	42	3.80	7	2	4	0	87.7	77	44	37	53	6	49
RP		Randy Gumpert	32	40	4.75	5	12	0	6	155.3	165	76	82	58	15	48
RP	*	Mickey Haefner	37	24	5.73	1	6	0	2	70.7	83	49	45	45	11	17
	*	Bob Kuzava	27	10	5.68	1	3	0	1	44.3	43	28	28	27	5	21
		Lou Kretlow	29	11	3.80	0	0	0	0	21.3	17	13	9	27	1	14
	*	Jack Bruner	25	9	3.65	0	0	0	0	12.3	7	6	5	14	0	8
	*	Marv Rotblatt	22	2	6.23	0	0	0	0	8.7	11	7	6	5	2	6
		John Perkovich	26	1	7.20	0	0	0	0	5.0	7	4	4	1	3	3
		Gus Keriazakos	18	1	19.29	0	1	0	0	2.3	7	5	5	5	0	1
		Bill Connelly	25	2	11.57	0	0	0	0	2.3	5	3	3	1	1	0
		Charlie Cuellar	32	2	33.75	0	0	0	0	1.3	6	6	5	3	0	1

* * * * *

ST. LOUIS BROWNS NOTES

Ballpark:	Sportsman's Park
Manager:	Zack Taylor
Runs Scored:	684
Runs Allowed:	916
Total Attendance:	247,131

TEAM BATTING

Pos	Player	AG	G	AB	R	H	2B	3B	HR	RBI	BB	SO	BA
C	Sherm Lollar	25	126	396	55	111	22	3	13	65	64	25	.280
1B	Don Lenhardt	27	139	480	75	131	22	6	22	81	90	94	.273
2B	Owen Friend	23	119	372	48	88	15	2	8	50	40	68	.237
3B	Bill Sommers	27	65	137	24	35	5	1	0	14	25	14	.255

Pos		Player	AG	G	AB	R	H	2B	3B	HR	RBI	BB	SO	BA
SS		Tom Upton	23	124	389	50	92	5	6	2	30	52	45	.237
OF	*	Dick Kokos	22	143	490	77	128	27	5	18	67	88	73	.261
OF	*	Ray Coleman	28	117	384	54	104	25	6	8	55	32	37	.271
OF		Ken Wood	25	128	369	42	83	24	0	13	62	38	58	.225
		Roy Sievers	23	113	370	46	88	20	4	10	57	34	42	.238
		Snuffy Stirnweiss	31	93	326	32	71	16	2	1	24	51	49	.218
	*	Hank Arft	28	98	280	45	75	16	4	1	32	46	48	.268
		Les Moss	25	84	222	24	59	6	0	8	34	26	32	.266
	*	Jim Delsing	24	69	209	25	55	5	2	0	15	20	23	.263
		Billy DeMars	24	61	178	25	44	5	1	0	13	22	13	.247
		Leo Thomas	26	35	121	19	24	6	0	1	9	20	14	.198
		Frankie Gustine	30	9	19	1	3	1	0	0	2	3	8	.158
		Ned Garver	24	51	91	13	26	4	0	1	10	8	9	.286
		Al Widmar	25	36	67	1	10	2	0	0	4	3	22	.149
		Stubby Overmire	31	31	48	3	8	0	1	0	8	12	2	.167
		Dick Starr	29	33	36	3	5	0	0	0	1	1	16	.139
	*	Cliff Fannin	26	33	34	6	6	1	0	0	2	0	6	.176
		Harry Dorish	28	30	31	3	5	2	0	0	2	6	8	.161
		Don Johnson	23	25	29	0	2	0	0	0	1	1	6	.069
		Duane Pillette	27	27	22	2	3	1	0	0	0	2	5	.136
	*	Joe Ostrowski	33	9	18	2	4	3	0	0	4	4	7	.222
	#	Tommy Fine	35	16	12	4	4	2	0	0	0	0	5	.333
		Cuddles Marshall	25	28	12	2	4	0	0	0	0	0	5	.333
	*	Jack Bruner	25	13	10	0	0	0	0	0	0	2	5	.000
		Tom Ferrick	35	16	4	1	1	0	0	0	0	0	1	.250
		Lou Kretlow	29	10	3	0	0	0	0	0	0	0	1	.000
		Sid Schacht	32	9	2	2	0	0	0	0	0	1	0	.000
		Ed Albrecht	21	2	1	0	0	0	0	0	0	0	0	.000
		Ribs Raney	27	1	1	0	0	0	0	0	0	0	1	.000

TEAM PITCHING

Pos		Player	AG	G	ERA	W	L	SV	CG	IP	H	R	ER	BB	HR	SO
SP		Ned Garver	24	37	3.39	13	18	0	22	260.0	264	120	98	108	18	85
SP		Al Widmar	25	36	4.76	7	15	4	8	194.7	211	115	103	74	16	78
SP	*	Stubby Overmire	31	31	4.19	9	12	0	8	161.0	200	89	75	45	11	39
SP		Cliff Fannin	26	25	6.53	5	9	1	3	102.0	116	82	74	58	18	42
RP		Cuddles Marshall	25	28	7.88	1	3	1	0	53.7	72	52	47	51	1	24
RP		Duane Pillette	27	24	7.09	3	5	2	1	73.7	104	62	58	44	6	18
RP		Harry Dorish	28	29	6.44	4	9	0	4	109.0	162	90	78	36	13	36
RP		Tom Ferrick	35	16	4.12	1	3	2	0	24.0	24	15	11	7	2	6
		Dick Starr	29	12	5.02	7	5	2	4	123.7	140	83	69	74	11	30
		Don Johnson	23	25	6.09	5	6	1	4	96.0	126	72	65	55	14	31
	*	Joe Ostrowski	33	9	2.51	2	4	0	2	57.3	57	22	16	7	2	15
		Tommy Fine	35	15	8.10	0	1	0	0	36.7	53	38	33	25	6	6
	*	Jack Bruner	25	13	4.63	1	2	1	0	35.0	36	21	18	23	4	16
		Lou Kretlow	29	9	11.93	0	2	0	0	14.3	25	19	19	18	2	10
		Sid Schacht	32	8	16.03	0	0	0	0	10.7	24	22	19	14	5	7
		Ed Albrecht	21	2	5.40	0	1	0	0	6.7	6	7	4	7	0	1
		Russ Bauers	36	1	4.50	0	0	0	0	2.0	6	4	1	1	0	0
	*	Bill Kennedy	29	1	0.00	0	0	0	0	2.0	1	1	0	2	0	1
		Ribs Raney	27	1	4.50	0	1	0	0	2.0	2	2	1	2	0	2
	*	Lou Sleater	23	1	0.00	0	0	0	0	1.0	0	0	0	0	0	1

* * * * *

PHILADELPHIA ATHLETICS NOTES

Ballpark:	Shibe Park
Manager:	Connie Mack
Runs Scored:	670
Runs Allowed:	913
Total Attendance:	309,805

TEAM BATTING

Pos		Player	AG	G	AB	R	H	2B	3B	HR	RBI	BB	SO	BA
C		Mike Guerra	37	87	252	25	71	10	4	2	26	16	12	.282
1B	*	Ferris Fain	29	151	522	83	147	25	4	10	83	133	26	.282
2B		Billy Hitchcock	33	115	399	35	109	22	5	1	54	45	32	.273
3B		Bob Dillinger	31	84	356	55	110	21	9	3	41	31	20	.309
SS		Eddie Joost	34	131	476	79	111	12	3	18	58	103	68	.233
OF		Sam Chapman	34	144	553	93	139	20	6	23	95	68	79	.251
OF	*	Elmer Valo	29	129	446	62	125	16	5	10	46	82	22	.280
OF	*	Paul Lehner	29	114	427	48	132	17	5	9	52	32	33	.309
		Kermit Wahl	27	89	280	26	72	12	3	2	27	30	30	.257
	*	Wally Moses	39	88	265	47	70	16	5	2	21	40	17	.264
		Pete Suder	34	77	248	34	61	10	0	8	35	23	31	.246
		Joe Tipton	28	64	184	15	49	5	1	6	20	19	16	.266
	*	Barney McCosky	33	66	179	19	43	10	1	0	11	22	12	.240
		Joe Astroth	27	39	110	11	36	3	1	1	18	18	3	.327
		Bob Wellman	24	11	15	1	5	0	0	1	1	0	3	.333
		Roberto Ortiz	35	6	14	1	1	0	0	0	3	0	3	.071
		Gene Markland	30	5	8	2	1	0	0	0	0	3	0	.125
		Ben Guintini	30	3	4	0	0	0	0	0	0	0	1	.000
		Bob Rinker	29	3	3	0	1	0	0	0	0	0	0	.333
	*	Lou Brissie	26	46	87	5	15	1	0	0	7	3	4	.172
		Alex Kellner	25	36	80	5	16	1	0	0	3	4	13	.200
		Bobby Shantz	24	37	66	4	11	1	0	1	4	6	10	.167
		Hank Wyse	32	41	59	4	9	0	0	0	4	1	14	.153
		Bob Hooper	28	45	56	4	7	2	0	1	8	0	21	.125
		Carl Scheib	23	50	52	6	13	0	1	1	6	1	9	.250
		Dick Fowler	29	11	26	2	5	0	0	0	2	0	1	.192
		Joe Coleman	27	15	17	2	1	0	0	1	1	2	5	.059
	*	Joe Murray	29	8	11	0	0	0	0	0	0	0	3	.000
		Johnny Kucab	30	4	9	0	1	0	0	0	1	1	1	.111

Pos		Player	AG	G	AB	R	H	2B	3B	HR	RBI	BB	SO	BA
		Moe Burtschy	28	9	5	2	0	0	0	0	0	2	1	.000
		Harry Byrd	25	6	2	0	0	0	0	0	0	0	1	.000
		Ed Klieman	32	5	1	0	0	0	0	0	0	0	0	.000

TEAM PITCHING

Pos		Player	AG	G	ERA	W	L	SV	CG	IP	H	R	ER	BB	HR	SO
SP	*	Lou Brissie	26	46	4.02	7	19	8	15	246.0	237	127	110	117	22	101
SP	*	Alex Kellner	25	36	5.47	8	20	2	15	225.3	253	157	137	112	28	85
SP	*	Bobby Shantz	24	36	4.61	8	14	0	6	214.7	251	122	110	85	18	93
SP		Hank Wyse	32	41	5.85	9	14	0	4	170.7	192	121	111	87	16	33
CL		Bob Hooper	28	45	5.02	15	10	5	3	170.3	181	108	95	91	15	58
RP		Carl Scheib	23	43	7.22	3	10	3	1	106.0	138	96	85	70	13	37
		Dick Fowler	29	11	6.48	1	5	0	2	66.7	75	52	48	56	7	15
		Joe Coleman	27	15	8.50	0	5	0	2	54.0	74	54	51	50	9	12
	*	Joe Murray	29	8	5.70	0	3	0	0	30.0	34	20	19	21	1	8
		Johnny Kucab	30	4	3.46	1	1	0	2	26.0	29	10	10	8	4	8
		Moe Burtschy	28	9	7.11	0	1	0	0	19.0	22	16	15	21	2	12
		Harry Byrd	25	6	16.88	0	0	0	0	10.7	25	20	20	9	3	2
		Ed Klieman	32	5	9.53	0	0	0	0	5.7	10	6	6	2	0	0
		Les McCrabb	35	2	27.00	0		0	0	1.3	7	4	4	0	0	2

Useful Bibliography

Dickson, Paul. *Baseball's Greatest Quotations*. Harper Perennial, 1992.

Halberstam, David. *Summer of '49. Perennial Classics, 2002.*

Hawkins, Jim and Ewald, Dan. *The Detroit Tigers Encyclopedia*. Sports Publishing L.L.C., 2003.

Pattison, Mark and Raglin, David. *Detroit Tigers: Lists and More*. Wayne State University Press, 2002.

Pietrusza, David, Silverman, Matthew, Gershman, Michael. *The Baseball Encyclopedia*. Sport Classic Books, 2003.

Wakabayashi, H. Clark. *The Little Big Book of Baseball*. Welcome Books, 2006.

Will, George. *Men At Work: The Craft of Baseball*. Harper Perennial, 1991.

Williams, Ted and Underwood, John. *The Science of Hitting*. A Fireside Book, 1986.

978-0-595-41849-7
0-595-41849-X

Printed in the United States
75250LV00006B/131